FAMILY AND
MARITAL THERAPY

FAMILY AND MARITAL THERAPY

A TRANSACTIONAL APPROACH

James E. Lantz, M.S.W.

Ohio State University School of Nursing and College of Social Work;
North Central Community Mental Health Center;
Formerly at Southwest Community Mental Health Center, Columbus, Ohio

Foreword by Grayce M. Sills, R.N., Ph.D.

Professor and Director of Graduate Psychiatric–Mental Health Nursing Program,
The Ohio State University, Columbus, Ohio

APPLETON-CENTURY-CROFTS / New York

Copyright © 1978 by APPLETON-CENTURY-CROFTS
A Publishing Division of Prentice-Hall, Inc.

78   79   80   81   82   /   10   9   8   7   6   5   4   3   2   1

Prentice-Hall International, Inc., London
Prentice-Hall of Australia, Pty. Ltd., Sydney
Prentice-Hall of India Private Limited, New Delhi
Prentice-Hall of Japan, Inc., Tokyo
Prentice-Hall of Southeast Asia (Pte.) Ltd., Singapore
Whitehall Books Ltd., Wellington, New Zealand

Library of Congress Cataloging in Publication Data
Lantz, James E., 1943–
    Family and marital therapy, a transactional approach.
    Bibliography: p. 209
    Includes index.
    1. Family psychotherapy. 2. Marital psychotherapy. I. Title.
RC488.5.L36   616.8'915   78-19186
ISBN 0-8385-2521-0

Text design: Edmée Froment

PRINTED IN THE UNITED STATES OF AMERICA

In Memory of Mary Weibling
Who Worked with Families for over Thirty Years

Contents

Preface

This book is written primarily for the beginning practitioner in marital and family therapy. Its goal is to provide such practitioners (undergraduate and graduate nurses, social workers, counsellors, family physicians, psychiatrists, psychologists, mental health technicians, and ministers) with an introductory, transactional view of family and marital processes as well as an initial understanding of intervention methods. This book is not meant to replace training or supervision, but to provide a place to start in the development of a transactional, family therapy knowledge base.

Throughout this book I have tried to use the word "therapist" when referring to the professional person working with the family group. In some instances the use of this term has been awkward and I have used the term "he" when such usage follows the context of what has been stated previously. This is done with the recognition that the family therapist can be of either the female or male gender. Also, I have used the terms "open" and "closed" system as relative terms; no system is completely "open" or "closed." Finally, I have used the symbol $-S +0$ to mean crossing out the self for the sake of the other; the symbol $+S -0$ to mean crossing out the other for the sake of the self; the symbol $-S -0$ to mean crossing out both the self and the other; and the symbol $+S +0$ to mean crossing out neither the self nor the other.

JEL

Acknowledgments

I wish to thank Margaret Carnine, R.N., Managing Editor of the *Journal of Psychiatric Nursing and Mental Health Services* for granting permission to reprint segments of "Family Therapy: Using A Transactional Approach," which first appeared in that journal. Chapters One, Two, and Three are an expansion of that article. Thanks to Beatrice Saunders, Editor of *Social Work* and the National Association of Social Workers for granting permission to use segments of "Co-therapy Approach in Family Therapy," which originally appeared in that journal. Chapter Ten is an expansion of that article.

I wish to thank my social and professional network that includes: Pam Argus, Charles Bollinger, Mary Jane Fox, Jim Gebhart, Jim Gibson, Marti Knisley, Ed Krug, Jean and George Lantz, Bev Lenahan, Fran McGhee, Jane and Don Osuga, Mike Preston, Don Tosi, Dorothy Turner, and Gary Young. These individuals have offered me much direction, encouragement, and support.

Most importantly, I wish to thank Ernest Andrews, Walt Pillow, Grayce Sills, and Kay Werk. Ernest Andrews originally introduced me to the field of Family Therapy while I was attending graduate school at Ohio State University. I consider myself most fortunate to have obtained training and supervision with Ernie whom I believe to be one of the most skilled family therapists in the country. I consider Ernie to be my most important influence in developing my own style and approach. Walt Pillow was my field instructor and advisor in graduate school. He taught me how to learn and that the self is the professional's most important tool. I am still using the concepts that Walt originally helped me discover. I wish to thank Grayce Sills who has taught me a great deal through both her intellect and her presence as a person. I appreciate her providing the Foreword for this book. Finally, I wish to thank Kay Werk, my most special friend. Kay has taught me more about the functional relationship than anyone else, simply by being herself.

Foreword

Men, women, children, humankind—all of us have our roots and our shaping in family structures and processes. The most pervasive and profound experiences of our lives are enacted in the loci of our families. Most of what is joyous and grievous, bane and blessing, pain and pleasure, is experienced first in families. Thus, persons bond themselves to themselves and to one another. This book focuses, then, on human communication as a bonding process in family life.

The author deals with family and marital troubles and their remedy. Lantz's approach is conceptually based and, at the same time, is eminently pragmatic. The work of families is transacted through communication processes. Thus, it is through these lenses that Lantz frames the work for those who would seek to facilitate the bonding in families.

There is great need for such an approach to working with the problems of marital and family life. For example, a recent article in "TV Guide" referred to the power of that medium to inform and educate in matters related to health. Of great interest was this comment:

At the present rate, 35 to 40 percent of all new marriages will end in divorce. So? Aren't unhappily married couples likely to be happier after they split? According to the latest studies, the odds are against it. Yet what can be done? There are simply not enough trained professionals to deal with even a small proportion of marriages in trouble, especially when every couple perceives its marital problems as unique. But as Gail Sheehy's best-selling book *Passages* demonstrates, they aren't really unique, and might be helped by some mass counseling on television.

What is of most interest in the above quotation is the implicit assumption that it is (or must be) well known that what needs to be done to "fix," "repair," "mend," or "straighten" problems in marriages and families indeed occurs in dyadic and multidyadic relationships. Clearly, if these remedies were well known and well tested, the promise of the medium of television might, as the author quoted above, be realizable. But would it be desirable?

However, it is this perspective—that of focusing on the relationship rather than on the psyche—that is the major contribution of this book to the burgeoning literature of family therapy. Particularly those who work in community mental health settings should find Lantz's approach useful and worth testing in clinical practice. The potential value for this society in strengthening the healthy functioning of family life is clearly a priority for all human service professionals. This book is a significant addition to the armamentarium of people who would seek to serve the purpose of aiding families to become healthy and functional.

GRAYCE M. SILLS, R.N., Ph.D.
Professor and Director of Graduate
Psychiatric-Mental Health Nursing Program
The Ohio State University, Columbus, Ohio

Introduction

Why See
the Family Group?

During the early 1950s, a number of individuals started viewing emotional disturbance as not just a reflection of the individual's internal difficulties, but also as a reflection of the relationship difficulties between the individual and his social situation. As a result of this new way of looking at emotional disturbance, a great deal of new data became available to the practitioner. For example, in various child guidance centers around the country, therapists started seeing the child with his parents. This new form of interviewing revealed new information and data. A child with problems of impulse control, who was previously diagnosed and treated in terms of his internal difficulties, could now be seen as a child who is responding to contradictory messages or commands sent to him by his parents. Previously unexplained behavior became much more understandable. As a result of this new approach to viewing human behavior, more and more practitioners began to see the total family as the primary unit of therapeutic attention. The individual exhibiting emotional or behavioral problems began to be seen as a reflection or a signal of disturbance within that individual's family group (Andrews, 1974; Satir, 1964).

For example, Mrs. Owens called a mental health center asking for help. She stated that her seven-year-old son refused to go to school. When she took him to school, he became ill and vomited. Mrs. Owens wanted the mental health center to help her son face "his problem." Mrs. Owens, Mr. Owens, and Johnny were scheduled to see a family therapist. In the initial interview, the family therapist discovered that Mr. and Mrs. Owens spent very little time together. Mr. Owens worked long hours, was involved in a number of community activities, and left Mrs. Owens and Johnny to be by themselves most of the time. Mr. Owens enjoyed being away from home as he viewed Mrs. Owens as depressed and sad. Mrs. Owens stated that she wanted Johnny to go to school, but admitted that she hated to face the day without his company.

During the initial interview, the family therapist helped Mrs. Owens express her feelings of loneliness and her desire to spend more time with her husband. Mr. Owens was able to openly express his frustration at his wife, who had "let herself go." Mr. and Mrs. Owens expressed a desire to work out some of their problems and contracted with the therapist for marital counseling. The therapist instructed Mrs. Owens to take Johnny to school even if he did become "sick."

Within five weeks, Johnny was happily attending school, Mrs. Owens had stopped most of her depression, and Mr. Owens was becoming a more active part of the family. Mrs. Owens was comfortable facing the day without her son.

The previous illustration is meant to highlight the point that an individual exhibiting emotional disturbance often is signaling a problem in the functioning of the total family group. In this instance, Johnny's "school phobia problem" also reflected a marital problem between husband and wife. Mrs. Owens reacted to her own and her husband's emotional distance by trying to meet her needs for human intimacy primarily through her son. She sent her son the contradictory message, "go to school, but don't go to school," and the son responded by getting sick when he attempted to leave his mother alone. When the marital pair recognized and began to work on their mutual problem of distance and isolation, Johnny felt free to go to school. If the case had been handled in terms of "Johnny's problem," there is a good possibility that the child might have accepted the label "sick" and developed even more symptoms in the following years.

Seeing the family group as the primary unit of attention has made sense to a significant number of therapists. Family therapy is presently the fastest growing therapeutic modality. As a result of this tremendous growth, there appears within the literature a wide variety of techniques, methods, and points of view. This variety seems beneficial to me, but has created some problems. One problem is that the beginning family therapist often becomes confused about this variety and variation. The goal of this book is to present a place to start. I hope to present a family therapy framework and practical guide for the beginning family therapy practitioner. I hope that this book will facilitate even more interest in family therapy and that it will provide the beginner with some helpful, first advice.

FAMILY AND
MARITAL THERAPY

1

The Family Group: Structure and Communication

The family can be defined as a group of individuals who share a common biological history and/or a future. In most instances, the individual's family is primarily responsible for his socialization and what he has learned about himself and his view of the world. We bring to every new situation a history of thoughts, feelings, attitudes, and behaviors that primarily were learned through our past interactions with our own family group.

The family group has great potential as both an agent for growth and an agent for despair. The family group is a relationship system that can create conditions for maximum human happiness and also, at times, can be a stumbling block for human autonomy, growth, and intimacy. Although it is possible for the individual to grow and develop without the help of his family group, such growth can be difficult if one's family system views such change as threatening or unacceptable.

Sections of this chapter appeared in "Family Therapy: Using a Transactional Approach." *Journal of Psychiatric Nursing* 15(4):17–22, April 1977, and are reprinted with the permission of Margaret Carnine, R.N., Managing Editor.

The family group is a relationship system that can have great influence over all of our thoughts, feelings, and behavior.

THE FAMILY GROUP AS A RELATIONSHIP SYSTEM

The family group can best be understood as a relationship system within which each member has an influence upon all the other members and within which all members have an influence upon each individual member. Satir uses a rubber band model to illustrate this mutual influence phenomenon found in every family group (Satir, 1972). If one takes four paper clips (one for father, one for mother, one for son, one for daughter) and connects each paper clip with rubber bands, one constructs a model that is fairly illustrative of the family group system (Fig. 1).

After the model is built, if the paper clip representing father is moved, all the other paper clips representing other family members will also move. Any movement or change in one member of the family will then, because of the interlocking nature of family relationships, be felt by all the other members of the family system.

For example, Bill, an 18-year-old freshman at a local university, contacted a mental health center asking for individual counseling. Bill's goals for therapy included becoming more independent and feeling less anxious in social groups. Bill stated that he had always been a loner, felt very uneasy when away from his family, and had always counted on his parents for support in most new or unfamiliar situations. Bill quickly made a number of gains through individual counseling. He became more outgoing, made new friends, and developed an increased capacity to take risks in his interpersonal relationships. Bill was happy with his new-found strength and found the courage to start dating girls. He could hardly wait for quarter vacation break so that he could return home to show his family the stronger, more independent Bill.

Bill returned from his quarter break visit in a very unhappy state. He felt depressed, guilty, and was horrified to find that his parents were not happy with his newly discovered personal strength. Bill reported that his mother became upset when he tried to do things for himself and that his father was angry because he felt that Bill no longer "appreciated all the things we have done for you." Bill felt guilty in spite of his awareness that he had done nothing wrong. Fortunately, Bill was able to understand that his parent's need to be needed did not require him to continue his role of "emotional cripple." Bill was able to continue acting in a more autonomous way. He later discovered that

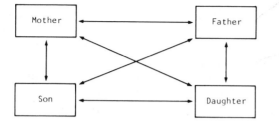

Figure 1. *The mutual influence phenomenon (Adapted from Satir, 1972)*

his parents could adjust to his newly won independence and eventually even developed a better relationship with each other since they no longer "had" to care for him.

COMMUNICATION IN THE FAMILY GROUP

In most societies, the family group provides the individual the opportunity to be with at least one significant other in a meaningful relationship. In order for this relationship system to be functional and enjoyable, the relationship members must find ways of meeting what Satir calls, "basic psychological needs." According to Satir, any functional relationship must meet the relationship members' needs for intimacy, production, and sense-order (Satir, 1972). The psychological need for sense-order means that the relationship members must be able to predict or make sense out of the relationships that make up their family environment.

For example, Bob, who recently married Betty, is trying very hard to make a go at a new business. As a result, he thinks that he must work long hours. At times, Betty complains that Bob is away from home too much. And at other times, she complains that he comes home too early and might have missed an opportunity to make a sale. He is anxious, but does not want to talk it out, as he thinks that talking might start a fight. Bob's anxiety is a result of his not knowing what to expect. As long as his need for sense and order is not met within the context of his relationship, he will probably continue to feel anxiety.

The psychological need for production means that the relationship members each have a desire to make a contribution to the other members of the family group. When the individual, for one reason or another, cannot make a contribution or does not have his contribution recognized by significant others, the individual generally feels some degree of depression and/or despair.

For example, John, who has been a steady hard-working individual for over fifteen years, has always felt good about his ability to meet the financial needs of his family. Recently, he had an accident that prevents him from going to work. Joyce has started working, as John's compensation payments are not high enough to meet all of their financial obligations. John feels unhappy about his present inability to work. He believes that he has somehow let his family down. He would like to start doing some things for the family such as shopping and errands, but Joyce tells him, "That's not your job", and "You really don't need to, dear." Joyce is trying to be helpful by doing as much as possible to let John recuperate, even though she realizes that it would help if John could do some of the errands. John and Joyce never talk about the problem and Joyce wonders why John feels so down.

The psychological need for intimacy means that all human beings have a desire for emotional closeness with another that allows them to know each others full range of human uniqueness (Andrews, 1974). One generally first experiences this type of relationship in his family of origin. Without this intimate and trusting sense of closeness, the individual may not develop confidence in his ability to negotiate new relationships outside of his original family group. This problem then reappears as the individual starts his or her own family and is then generally passed on to the next generation (Paul and Paul, 1975).

When the family as a group meets the psychological needs of its members, those members grow and develop in a functional way (Satir, 1964). When the family as a group does not meet the psychological needs of its individual members, at least one family member will generally develop a signal of family system dysfunction. Such signals may take the form of anxiety, anger, depressions, and/or somatic complaints (Andrews, 1974), and in turn may increasingly inhibit future family communication sequences. Figure 2 illustrates this dysfunctional circular family process.

It is impossible for a family group to meet its members' needs for intimacy, sense-order, and production without clear, precise, and functional communication (Satir, 1964). Almost all disturbed families exhibit dysfunctional communication and almost all undisturbed families exhibit functional communication (Andrews, 1974; Satir, 1964). Functional communication is the vehicle through which the family group provides its members the opportunity to meet their psychological needs (Andrews, 1974). It therefore follows that, in order to help a disturbed family group meet its members' psychological needs, the family therapist must give some time and attention toward helping the family group improve the quality of its communication

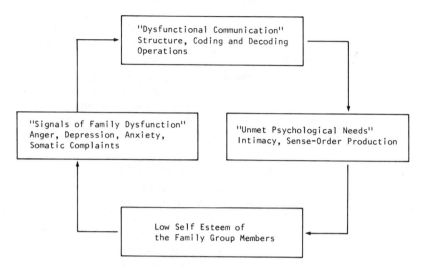

Figure 2. *The development of family dysfunction signals (Lantz, 1977)*

processes. In order to understand the various elements within the complicated family communication process, it is helpful to view such communication elements in their simplest form, the dyadic group.

ELEMENTS OF COMMUNICATION IN THE DYADIC GROUP

A dyadic group includes the thoughts, feelings, and behavior of two human beings and also the relationship that results from the combined thinking, feeling, and behavior of those two human beings (Lantz, 1977). Internal behaviors such as thinking and feeling can be looked at as a self-communication process (Ellis, 1962). Self-communication processes are a way of evaluating or decoding the messages we receive from our social situation. Such evaluations and decoding operations can be viewed as functional when they are (1) based on an accurate understanding of the objective reality; (2) goal-producing; (3) life-preserving; and (4) are used to decrease significant personal and inter-personal conflict (Maultsby, 1975). External human behaviors (be-haviors that can be perceived by others) can be viewed as an output process of communicating to others. Such output coding communica-tions behaviors can be viewed as functional when they are clear, pre-cise, and congruent (Satir, 1964). Communicating clearly to others is important as it allows us to negotiate differences, develop mutual goals, and work together for shared relationship outcomes (Andrews, 1974). Communicating clearly to self (making accurate decoding evaluations) is important, as many of our emotions follow logically from such cognitive evaluations (Ellis, 1962). Figure 3 shows a dyadic group model that can be used as a practical guide for both assessment and intervention when viewing dyadic group communication processes. This model is an elaboration of an emotional analysis model developed by Ellis (1962) and a self-in-situation model developed by Mooney (1963).

A dyadic group relationship can become dysfunctional in a variety of ways. Messages become unclear and confusing because (1) they are being sent in an unclear way (A-output processes); (2) they are being evaluated and decoded inaccurately (B-decoding processes are confused); and (3) output and decoding processes are both confused and distorted (Lantz, 1977). Within the relationship, when messages and evaluations become continuously confused, the relationship members begin to increasingly experience anger, anxiety, depression, and somatic complaints (Andrews, 1974).

When a man and woman decide to form a marital relationship (which is a dyadic group), they bring with them patterns of cognitive distortion and ineffective methods of output communication. This always unique blend results initially in a marital style and later further develops into a family interactional style. Within any marital counseling session, the therapist can become aware of a repetitive marital transaction that represents the relationship problem resulting from the unique blend of that couple's decoding and coding communication distortions. With the addition of children, this repetitive dyadic transaction changes to become a repetitive family transaction that is equally reinforced and maintained by the total family group membership. The goal of family therapy can then be understood as a family group trans-

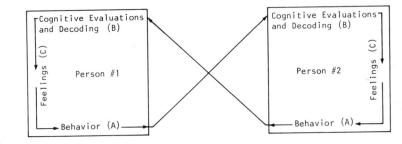

Figure 3. *The dyadic group model (Lantz, 1977)*

actional reshaping process. The family therapist can then be viewed as a facilitator who by professional interventive action helps the family reshape their dysfunctional repetitive group transactions (Lantz, 1977).

SOME COMMON TRANSACTIONAL STYLES

Satir has identified four common transactional styles (Satir, 1964). The first transactional style is when the individual continuously crosses out himself for the sake of another. This is similar to what Berne (1964) and Harris (1967) call an "I'm not OK, you're OK" transactional stance (Fig. 4).

The extreme form of this transactional style is suicide. In its milder forms, the individual evaluates and decodes most input from others in a self-effacing way. A fairly typical example of this stance is interactional martyrdom, which is illustrated in the following conversation:

JOHN:

Honey, I'm going out to play golf with Jack and Harry. I'll be home late for dinner. Is that okay with you?

MARY:

[*Deep sigh*] Well . . . it's okay, I guess. There are lots of things I should get done around the house. Whatever you want. It's okay . . . I guess.

In this example, Mary, who doesn't really want John to go play golf, doesn't manifest herself in a congruent way. She so desperately believes that she needs her husband's love and approval that she does

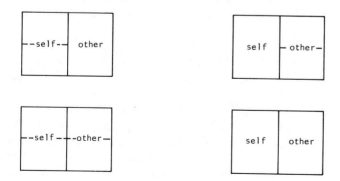

Figure 4. *Four transactional styles*

not take a chance on disagreeing or presenting her view due to the possibility that he will "not like it," or "leave," or "get mad at me." In the extreme forms of this interactional stance, the individual may even believe that "without my husband, wife, children, parents, or friends, I do not exist." Mary has fooled herself into believing that her husband's wants are more important than her own. On the other hand, John plays into the game by not commenting on Mary's incongruent communication and by not asking for further clarification. This dysfunctional transactional style may well lead to depression, resentment, anger, boring bedrooms, too many golf games, and an occasional child who resembles the milkman.

A second transactional style is when the individual continuously crosses out others for the sake of himself. This is similar to what Berne (1964) and Harris (1967) call an "I'm OK, you're not OK" transactional stance and is illustrated in Figure 4.

The extreme form of this transactional style is homicide. Such a stance is characterized by blaming, projection, and an inability to see the other person's point of view. Individuals who exhibit this type of transactional style often use anger and blame as a way of fending off depression, sadness, and despair. Their transactional style, designed to give momentary relief from emotional pain, often results in the individual provoking distance between himself and others, which in the long run does not represent a solution to the individual's problem.

A third common transactional style is when the individual continuously crosses out both himself and others. This style is similar to what Berne (1964) and Harris (1967) call an "I'm not OK, you're not OK" transactional stance (Fig. 4). The extreme form of this transactional stance is similar to schizophrenia. An individual who operates out of this transactional stance usually has low self esteem and also believes that others are equally worthless. This stance is characterized by isolation, withdrawal, and an outstanding ability of the individual to provoke emotional distance with others.

A fourth transactional style is when the individual crosses out neither himself nor others. This stance is similar to what Berne (1964) and Harris (1967) call an "I'm OK, you're OK" transactional stance (Fig. 4).

This transactional style is labeled by Satir (1964) as maturation. By maturation, Satir means "that state in which a given human being is fully in charge of himself" (Satir, 1964). She further elaborates by saying that "an individual exhibits maturation by having accurate perceptions about self and other, making choices based on those perceptions and by acknowledging those choices as being his own" (Satir,

1964). Maturation and responsibility for self can be measured in terms of sentence structure. Maturation is evident when the individual "can use the first person I, followed by an active verb and ending with a direct object" (Satir, 1964).

This fourth transactional style can be viewed as the goal of therapy. Such a transactional style allows the individual to be uniquely himself without disregarding the uniqueness of others, and allows individuals to meet the psychological needs of both themselves and significant others. Such a transactional style occurs only when the relationship pair both are able to make accurate decoding operations and send clear, precise, and congruent messages to others.

HOW THE TRANSACTIONAL STYLES CAN COMBINE

The four common transactional styles can be combined to produce five different relationship styles. The five styles are avoid-avoid, attack-avoid, attack-attack, intimacy, and the fifth style, which can be called the terminate or change relationship style. The avoid-avoid relationship occurs whenever (1) a $-S-O$ marries a $-S-O$, (2) a $-S+O$ marries a $-S-O$, or (3) a $-S+O$ marries a $-S+O$. The attack-avoid relationship occurs whenever (1) a$-S-O$ marries a $+S-O$ or (2) a $+S-O$ marries a $-S+O$. The attack-attack relationship occurs when a $+S-O$ marries a $+S-O$. Intimacy occurs only when a $+S+O$ marries a $+S+O$. The final type of relationship, called the termination or change relationship style, occurs whenever a $+S+O$ marries any of the other interactional types. It has been the author's experience that in this type of relationship, the $+S+O$ individual will terminate the relationship unless the other relationship member changes to engage in the $+S+O$ relationship style.

RECIPROCITY

Reciprocity can be defined as a process in which the relationship members reinforce their own and each other's transactional style. If the transactional style being reinforced is functional, then the process of reciprocity can also be viewed as functional. If the transactional style being reinforced is dysfunctional, then the reciprocity process can also be viewed as dysfunctional. Much of family psychotherapy (which can be viewed as a transactional reshaping process) is geared toward interrupting, challenging, and changing the reciprocity process that occurs within the dysfunctional family group (Lantz, 1977). The following conversation illustrates one dysfunctional reciprocity process that can occur.

MOTHER:
> You make me so mad. I get so sick of your attitude. You drive me up a wall.

DAUGHTER:
> I do not. It's your fault. If you showed more trust, I wouldn't get so mad.

FATHER:
> Show some respect for your mother. You're making her a nervous wreck.

MOTHER:
> If you spent more time with her, she wouldn't be so bad. You're both driving me crazy.

In this conversation, mother, father, and daughter disagree about "who done it," but also, unfortunately they all agree that "someone else did it to them." Mother, father, and daughter all reinforce each other's transactional style and low level of maturation. As long as the family group as a system believes that blame is the answer, they will continue to reinforce this reciprocal "who done it" process which will result in what Watzlawick, Beaven, and Jackson (1967) call "a game without end." Such a game insures that the family group does not consistently provide for its members' needs. As a result, at least one member of the family group will, in most instances, begin to exhibit or develop symptoms.

Reciprocity is often a subtle process. For example, in the Willis family, Bob (the father) and Peg (the mother) have for years been unhappy in their marital relationship. Usually this dissatisfaction is expressed through mutual avoidance. However, from time to time, the resentment surfaces and there is talk of divorce. When this happens, Ben (the oldest son) runs away. Peg and Bob then forget their differences and concentrate on finding their son. After Ben returns home, Bob and Peg return to their pattern of mutual avoidance. This family process is maintained both by the marital pair and the son. The son helps the parents avoid their conflict by running away. The parents use the son's behavior to insure that nothing gets settled. In this sense, both the parents and the son reinforce the family rule that conflict is to be avoided. This pattern will continue until the son reaches maturity and leaves home. At that point, the parents may continue the process with another child who is next in line. This process will continue until the parents decide to talk things out even if their children run away.

FAMILY STRUCTURE

Family communication includes not only the combined coding and decoding operations of the total family group (i.e., their transactional style), but also the flow and direction of the various family transactions (Lantz, 1977). Family structure refers to who is communicating what to whom. Although each family group will develop a family structure that reflects its own uniqueness, there are some structures that seem to work better than others. Functional families (families that meet their individual member's psychological needs) tend to develop a balanced family structure as opposed to an unbalanced family structure (Glick and Kessler, 1974).

In the Smally family, Mr. Smally meets his emotional needs through drinking. Mrs. Smally feels left out and alone and she handles her feelings by yelling at Mr. Smally and by asking her oldest son John for emotional support. John recognizes his mother's pain (not father's) and feels an obligation to listen to her when she complains about the father. On the other hand, John resents his task, and feels angry when he "has" to listen to Mom rather than do other age-appropriate activities. The Smally family can be considered an unbalanced family structure because the parents do not meet each other's psychological needs through the marital relationship. The mother involves her oldest son in most of her intimacy need-reduction transactions while at the same time pushing father away. Father is content to isolate himself and therefore reinforces the dysfunctional pattern. The Smally family structure can be illustrated as in Figure 5.

In Figure 5, the squiggly line represents what various family therapists have called a generational boundary line (Andrews, 1974; Satir, 1964). When family members start to continuously cross over the generational boundary line to meet most of their psychological needs, problems usually start to develop in at least one family member. An alternative family system structure is the balanced family group. In the balanced family group, the marital pair help each other meet their psychological needs through the use of functional communication. Such a balanced family system can be illustrated as in Figure 6.

In the balanced family system, the marital dyad is functional and the marital relationship members do not need to look outside of that relationship for the major portion of their psychological needs. In the

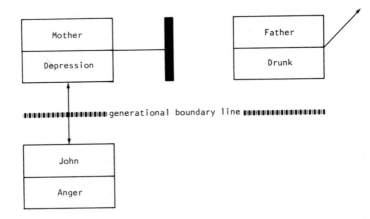

Figure 5. *An unbalanced family system*

unbalanced family system, the marital dyad generally communicates to each other in a dysfunctional way. As a result, the marital relationship members may begin to develop a pattern of looking outside of that relationship for their primary psychological need-meeting operations. If parents look to the children as their primary source of need satisfaction, the children are placed in a bind, as they are not yet developmentally ready for such a relationship. On the other hand, if one of the marital dyad looks to his or her own parents as their primary source of

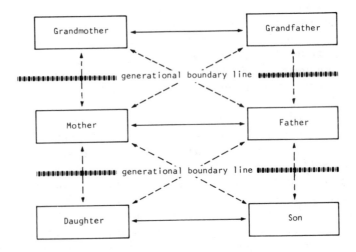

Figure 6. *A balanced family group*

need satisfaction, the marital member will be reinforcing himself for a lack of autonomy and independence. In addition, the marital member will also be placing himself in a position that is less than his developmental capacities would allow. Such generational boundary violations are felt throughout the family group due to the mutual influence phenomenon operating in all family systems. Such boundary violations usually set off a state of depression, anxiety, or other distress signals in at least one family member.

SUMMARY

The family group can be viewed and understood as a system in which each family member has influence upon all other family members and in which each individual member is influenced by all the other family members. Such a family system can be considered functional when it is able to meet its individual's psychological needs for intimacy,

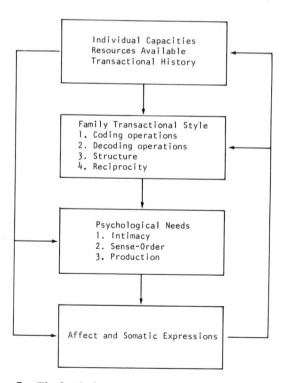

Figure 7.   *The family functioning cycle (Lantz, 1977)*

sense-order, and production. The functional family system is able to meet its member's psychological needs because all family members participate in a functional, repetitive family transactional style. Such a functional family transactional style includes accurate decoding operations, clear, precise, and congruent coding operations, and a balanced structure for the family communication and/or transactional flow. Figure 7 illustrates a family functioning cycle.

When individual emotional disturbance is understood as resulting from a dysfunctional repetitive family transactional process, then all forms of therapy can be viewed as being in some way a family group transactional, reshaping process. Although transactional reshaping can occur in a variety of ways, it is the author's opinion that such a transactional reshaping process can occur most efficiently when the family is viewed as the primary unit of therapeutic attention. With this framework in mind, the family group therapist will, in most instances, see the family together in a family group interview. However, the family therapist will also feel free to interview individuals, dyads, and other various family subsystems when the need so arises. Family therapy is an orientation and point of view rather than a given set of procedural operations (Haley, 1970). As a result, the family group therapist may at any given time use a variety of transactional reshaping strategies.

The following two chapters will describe and illustrate a few of the many possible reshaping procedures. Chapter 2 is primarily concerned with assessment, contracting, and the development of a therapeutic alliance. Chapter 3 will describe a number of change-stimulating strategies while Chapters 4, 5, and 6 will present illustrative interviews.

2

The Initial Stage of Family Therapy

Any consideration of family therapy should include the aspects of family assessment, developing a therapeutic alliance, developing a treatment contract, and the various change-facilitating activities. In practice, these four activities occur simultaneously, with the exception that the therapist may focus more upon relationship building and assessment in the initial stage. As a result, it is difficult to write about these four family therapy activities. On one hand, if the writer does not separate these categories of activity into some kind of meaningful order, the reader may respond with some resulting confusion. On the other hand, if the writer separates these activities, the reader may lose the true flavor of the family therapy process. My solution to this problem is to separate the categories. I hope that the reader will remember that the process is never so precise, and will be able to make maximum use of these distinctions, especially when combined with his or her own experiential learning.

Sections of this chapter appeared in "Family Therapy: Using a Transactional Approach." *Journal of Psychiatric Nursing* 15(4):17–22, April 1977, and are reprinted with the permission of Margaret Carnine, R.N., Managing Editor.

DEVELOPING A THERAPEUTIC ALLIANCE

Relationship building is of primary importance in the initial stage of family therapy. All families come to the therapist with a set of habitual transactional patterns that have been learned through repetition over a long period of time. The family is also in pain, and each member generally sees his or her own behavior as justified in view of that pain. Most dysfunctional transactional patterns not only contribute to the family's pain, but also are used and sometimes viewed by the family membership as a way of temporarily decreasing that emotional pain. As a result, the family may be frightened of change and will, as a group or system, resist such change. In order to help the family group avoid unnecessary resistance, the therapist attempts to make some sort of an initial contact or emotional alliance with each member of the family group. Such an emotional alliance can occur through the use of structure, emotional accommodation, the acceptance of symptoms, and various mimicking behaviors of the therapist.

STRUCTURE

One way to help decrease the family group's initial fear, anxiety, or resistance is for the therapist to provide the family with some initial structure (Satir, 1964). In such a structure, the therapist usually tells the family who the therapist is, what the therapist will be doing, what the therapist wants the family to do, and how the family can help in the process. Such a structural presentation is valuable, as it models clear communication, shows the family that the therapy process has a direction and a set of goals, and finally, helps the family meet its needs for sense, order, and production. Such a structural presentation is most effective when the therapist presents the structure through both content (talking about what will occur), and process (doing what has been talked about).

EMOTIONAL ACCOMMODATION

Emotional accommodation can be viewed as those internal processes that occur within the therapist that allow him or her to develop empathetic understanding for the family group and its individual members (Minuchin, 1974). Such emotional accommodation on the therapist's part is important, because if the family is to develop new, more functional patterns of interaction, they must also lose or change their previous dysfunctional patterns. Such a change implies risk. The family group generally will not take such a risk unless the family group membership trusts the therapist. Such initial trust will not develop unless the therapist is able to effectively communicate to the family some degree of empathy, concern, and understanding. Emotional accommodation on the part of the therapist helps the family group meet its needs for intimacy.

THE ACCEPTANCE OF SYMPTOMS

A third way in which the therapist can promote a therapeutic alliance is to accept the family's symptoms (Minuchin, 1974; Haley, 1976). Accepting symptoms can be viewed as both a method of developing initial trust and also as a method for producing change. For example, if a family therapist asks a teen-age family member who is sulking and acting difficult to show the therapist in the interview exactly what it is he or she does that the parents complain about and call sulking, the teen-ager is then in the position of having to either stop sulking (which is a change in the family interaction) or to take a compliment from the therapist for the excellent job he or she is doing to help the therapist understand. This second option will allow the client the initial experience of receiving warmth, compliments, and strokes from the family therapist. This in turn sets the stage for the adolescent to accept future warmth, which is a beginning in the development of trust.

MIMICKING BEHAVIORS OF THE THERAPIST

Mimicking behaviors are a direct result of emotional accommodation. When a therapist feels some concern for the various family members, his tone of voice, choice of words, and use of gestures may begin to take on a few of the family's characteristics (Minuchin, 1974). Mimicking behaviors are generally a nonverbal attempt on the part of the therapist to be with or understand the family without losing his or her own autonomy and differentiation. Such mimicking behaviors are generally picked up by the family on a nonverbal level and when received by the family group membership also provide a basis for beginning trust. Mimicking behaviors by the therapist are another way the therapist can help the family group members meet their needs for intimacy.

A CLINICAL ILLUSTRATION

The following conversation was recorded in an initial family group interview and illustrates a few ways in which the therapist can facilitate a therapeutic alliance in the initial stage of family therapy. This conversation illustrates all of the previously mentioned strategies except for the acceptance of symptoms.

[*Background noises*]

THERAPIST:
> Do we have enough chairs? Looks like we need one more. No, I guess we don't.

FATHER:
> That's enough.

THERAPIST:
> Okay, I'd like us to arrange them in a circle so we can all see each other.   (Structure)

[*Background noises, people moving chairs.*]

THERAPIST:
> Fine. I'd like to start off by learning names. Let's see. You're Mr. Young. You like to be called by your first name, or would you prefer Mr. Young?   (Structure)

FATHER:
> Bob.

THERAPIST:
> Fine. It's good to meet you. I'm Jim.
> [*Therapist and Father shake hands.*]

THERAPIST:
> Could you introduce me to your family?   (Structure)

FATHER:
> This is my wife, Sue.

THERAPIST:
> Nice meeting you. [*Shakes hands.*]

FATHER:
> And this is our daughter, Joyce.

THERAPIST:
> Hi, Joyce. [*Shakes hands.*]

THERAPIST:
> Okay, I'd like to find out a little about   (Structure)

each of you. Let's start with Joyce. That
okay with you?

DAUGHTER:

Yea.

THERAPIST:

Well, how old are you, Joyce?

DAUGHTER:

Thirteen.

THERAPIST:

And do you go to school?

DAUGHTER:

Yea.

THERAPIST:

Whereabouts?

DAUGHTER:

Jackson Junior High.

THERAPIST:

Let's see. You'd be in about the seventh
grade, right?

DAUGHTER:

Yea.

THERAPIST:

What kinds of things do you like to do?   (Emotional accommoda-
You know, for fun? Hobbies, that sort of   tion)
thing.

DAUGHTER:

I'm going to be a cheerleader.

THERAPIST:

You are!   (Emotional accommoda-
                                             tion)

DAUGHTER:

Yea.

THERAPIST:

You got a boyfriend?   (Mimicking behavior)

DAUGHTER:

Yea.

THERAPIST:

What's his name?

DAUGHTER:

Randy.

THERAPIST:

Is he good looking?   (Mimicking behavior)

DAUGHTER:
  Yea [*laughing*].
THERAPIST:
  No ugly old boyfriend for you.   (Mimicking behavior)
DAUGHTER:
  [*Laughing*] No.
THERAPIST:
  Okay, fine. Look, a little later, I'm going   (Structure)
  to ask you what you like best about your
  family and what you like least. Could you
  be thinking about that answer?
DAUGHTER:
  Okay.
THERAPIST:
  Fine.
THERAPIST:
  Okay, Mrs. Young. You prefer Sue or   (Emotional accommoda-
  Mrs. Young?   tion)

WIFE:
  Sue.
THERAPIST:
  Okay. What kinds of things are you in-
  terested in?

  [*Wife looks toward husband.*]

THERAPIST:
  No. I don't want you to ask him. I'm   (Structure)
  going to ask him the same question in just
  a moment. What kinds of things do you
  enjoy?
WIFE:
  Well, you know. Keeping house, raising
  Joyce. You know, the usual.
THERAPIST:
  Any interest outside of home and family?
  Clubs?
WIFE:
  Well, reading. I like to read.
THERAPIST:
  What kinds of things do you read?

WIFE:

Fiction.

THERAPIST:

Is that relaxing for you?   (Emotional accommodation)

WIFE:

Yea. I enjoy it a lot.

THERAPIST:

Okay Sue. I'm going to ask you the same   (Structure)
question I asked Joyce to think about.
Could you think about your answer?

WIFE:

Okay.

THERAPIST:

Good. Okay, Bob, how about you? What
kinds of things are you interested in?

FATHER:

Well, it's mostly work. Between work and
the family, I don't have time for much
else.

THERAPIST:

What do you do for a living?

FATHER:

I'm a salesman, and I'm on the road a lot.

THERAPIST:

Okay. When you do get home, what   (Structure)
kinds of things do you do?

FATHER:

Well, I do some of the work that needs to
be done—the grass, fixing things that get
broken.

THERAPIST:

You said you spent some time with your
wife and daughter. How do you spend
that time?

FATHER:

Lately, it's mostly been fighting.

THERAPIST:

Okay. Is that something you'd like to do   (Emotional accommoda-
less of?   tion and structure)

FATHER:

Yea, a lot less.

THERAPIST:

Okay. Let's see, Sue, you called originally   (Structure)
to set up the appointment. Could you tell
me how that came about?

WIFE:

Well, it's like Bob said. We've been fighting a lot and then Joyce ran away. So, we
just decided that things are getting out of
hand.

THERAPIST:

Okay. And how did you hear about me?

WIFE:

A neighbor of mine is one of your former
clients. She suggested you.

THERAPIST:

Okay, so this is something the three of
you decided upon?

WIFE:

Yea.

THERAPIST:

Okay. Joyce, is this something you   (Emotional accommoda-
wanted to do also?   tion)

DAUGHTER:

Yea. They suggested it.

THERAPIST:

But, you agreed that it might be a good   (Structure)
idea?

DAUGHTER:

Yea.

THERAPIST:

Okay, fine. Have you thought about the
question I said I was going to ask you?

DAUGHTER:

Yea.

THERAPIST:

Okay, good. What I'd like you to do is
turn toward either your father or your
mother. Which ever you choose and tell
them what it is you're most concerned
about in your family.

DAUGHTER:

Can't I tell you?

THERAPIST:

I'd like you to tell your parents cause you live with them, and it's important that you know what each other is concerned about.   (Structure)

DAUGHTER:

Well . . . [tearing up], they never listen.

THERAPIST:

Which one would you like to listen to you right now?   (Emotional accommodation)

DAUGHTER:

Dad.

THERAPIST:

Okay, Bob, Joyce has some things she'd like to talk about, but she's scared that you won't listen. Could you turn your chair around toward her and look at her so she knows you're listening?   (Structure)

[Father moves chair.]

THERAPIST:

Fine. That's fine.

ASSESSMENT

After the family therapist has made a beginning emotional alliance with each member of the family group, the therapist begins to focus primarily upon the assessment process. During the assessment process, the family therapist attempts to identify the specific repetitive dysfunctional transactional process that the family uses to create its difficulty in meeting its individual members' needs for intimacy, sense-order, and production. Within this assessment process, the therapist is interested in discovering the family's dysfunctional rules about coding and decoding operations as well as the flow and direction of the various family transactions. The following three questions can be kept in mind and used by the family therapist as an assessment guide. The three questions are the following:

1. Who is saying what to whom (refers to family structure).
2. How are the family members saying what to whom (refers to coding operations).
3. How are the family members hearing what has been said to whom (refers to family decoding operations) (Lantz, 1977).

WHO SAYS WHAT TO WHOM (FAMILY STRUCTURE)

As noted in Chapter 1, the question "Who is saying what to whom?" refers to family group structure. Families seem to develop symptom bearers whenever the marital dyad overinvolves one or more of the children in the marital relationship. Such dysfunctional cross-generational involvement can develop in a variety of ways. Three examples of dysfunctional cross-generational involvement are (1) the minor as marital therapist syndrome; (2) the minor as parental conflict weapon syndrome; and (3) the minor as a parental need-meeting device syndrome.

The Minor as Marital Therapist

In the minor as marital therapist syndrome, the child becomes frightened and anxious whenever the parents begin to openly manifest conflict. The child becomes anxious because he has generally learned from the parents that anger/conflict is a terrible thing to be avoided at all cost. As a result, whenever the parents begin to openly manifest conflict, the child begins to act out. Such acting out behaviors can include, among others, temper tantrums, psychosomatic illness, hallucinations, and running away. As soon as the child develops his or her symptom, the marital pair immediately drop the conflict, run to the child with sympathy and concern, and reward the child for his butting-in behavior. This process is reciprocal. The parents reward the child by giving it sympathy and concern for its symptom development and, at the same time, the parents are rewarded due to the fact that they no longer need to concentrate on (or for that matter, resolve) their own conflict. Both the parents and the child compatibly agree that conflict is a terrible thing, and each member of the family group will do his or her part to insure that "things don't get out of hand." This process can be interrupted, challenged, and changed with the help of a therapist who refuses to let the marital pair off the hook.

The Minor as Parental Conflict Weapon

In the minor as parental conflict weapon syndrome, one of the marital pair is generally dominant and/or aggressive, and the other is usually withdrawn and/or passive. In this process, the passive member of the marital pair is unwilling to openly express his or her resentment. As a result, the passive member involves one of the children in the marital "fight" by getting the child to act out toward the dominant spouse. For example:

DOMINANT WIFE:
> John, the kids have been terrible all day. I told them they weren't getting any dinner tonight.

PASSIVE HUSBAND:
> Yes, dear. I agree. You kids shouldn't treat your mother that way. But, before you go upstairs to bed without dinner, look at this nice candy father brought you for a present. Now, you take this candy and go upstairs. Oh, by the way, don't treat your mother so bad. [*Father smiles.*]

Again, this process can be interrupted, challenged, and changed by helping the marital dyad openly manifest and then resolve their marital conflict. Such marital conflict resolution can be accomplished by helping the passive member realize that an open expression of resentment will not bring the world to an end, but is instead, the beginning step toward negotiation for mutual outcome. It is also important that the therapist help the dominant spouse remember that the steamroller approach gives the passive mate additional excuses to continue his or her use of the children as a passive weapon of marital war.

The Minor as Parental Need-Meeting Device

In the minor as a parental need-meeting device syndrome, the parents have usually had a long history of marital dissatisfaction and marital despair. Usually, one of the marital dyad has withdrawn from the relationship and acts out this withdrawal through the use of long working hours, extramarital affairs, numerous community activities, and/or the excessive consumption of toxic drugs. The spouse is then left feeling isolated, angry, and depressed. The anger is expressed (not the hurt) which provokes further withdrawal on the part of the mate. At this point, the isolated spouse turns to one or more of the children for emotional nurturance and support. The child is then placed in the position of providing the isolated parent support, which is dysfunctional in that (1) the child does not have the developmental capacities to perform such a task; (2) the child should be using up his or her time and energy for age-appropriate activities; and (3) such a supportive task leads to unexpressed resentment and symptoms on the part of the child. Again, the successful resolution of this dysfunctional process generally depends upon the family's willingness and the therapist's ability to get the marital pair involved in talking out their problems.

HOW FAMILY MEMBERS SAY WHAT TO WHOM (FAMILY CODING OPERATIONS)

The question, "How are the family members saying what to whom?" refers to the family's rules about family communication coding operations. All families develop certain patterns or rules about output coding operations. Such rules are functional when they lead to coding operations that are clear, precise, and congruent (Satir, 1964). When the family group has developed output communication rules that lead to clear, precise, and congruent coding operations, the family is generally able to meet its individual members' needs for intimacy, sense-order, and production. Dysfunctional output communication rules lead to coding operations that are unclear, incongruent, and imprecise. Such dysfunctional coding operations insure that the family membership is unable to negotiate for mutual outcomes (Andrews, 1973). As a result, such a family usually develops a symptom bearer, as the family as a group is unable to meet its membership's psychological needs.

There are a number of dysfunctional family rules about coding operations that are typically found in families that produce at least one symptom bearer. Such dysfunctional family coding rules include (1) say what you don't mean, and mean what you don't say; (2) if you really loved me, I wouldn't have to ask; (3) the family secret; (4) nice people never disagree; (5) it's best to hint around; and (6) the generalizing general rule.

Say What You Don't Mean and Mean What You Don't Say

Many dysfunctional families develop communication coding rules where the members rather consistently say what they don't mean and mean what they don't say. For example:

WIFE:
Harry, don't you want to stop at the Brown Restaurant?

HUSBAND:
No, not really. I'd rather go to the Blue Lotus.

WIFE:

[*Angry tone*] You never want to do what I want. You're a selfish person.

HUSBAND:

[*Also angry*] What the hell did I do?

In this illustration, the wife asked her husband if he would like to go to a certain restaurant, but was meaning that she would like to go to that particular restaurant herself. In her own mind, she believed that she had communicated her meaning. As a result, she became angry when her husband replied to her content rather than the latent message. This in turn led to the wife's labeling her husband as selfish. The effects of such a distorted output coding operation are a mutual resentment and an inability of the relationship pair to negotiate for an outcome that would be satisfying to both.

If You Really Loved Me, I Wouldn't Have to Ask

In the if you really loved me, I wouldn't have to ask coding rule, the family members assume that the other family members have the ability to read each other's minds. Believing this basic assumption, the family members see no reason to ask for what they want. Since the other family members are not clairvoyant, the individual seldom gets what he wants and then interprets this result as meaning that "no one in this family loves me." After a period of time, the family members may decide to start asking for what they want. However, at this point, they interpret the improved outcome as not really meaning anything, since after all, "if you really loved me, I wouldn't have to ask." This dysfunctional coding rule allows the total family membership to "lose" no matter what the result.

The Family Secret

Many families compatibly agree never to discuss a certain subject or event. Such families will use a number of various silencing strategies if any single member attempts to violate the family rule. An example of this phenomenon often occurs in families whose membership includes an individual who is dying of a terminal disease. Very often the family will refuse to talk about the illness because they believe that talking about it will be too upsetting for the dying member or the younger children. The result of this decision is that the dying member begins to feel more and more isolated. In addition, the don't talk about it rule is often generalized to other areas of the family life. This process cannot help but have the effect of leaving the family group members up in the air, confused, and distant from each other during a period of time when they especially need each other's help.

Nice People Never Disagree

In this family rule, different opinions are interpreted as meaning that the family members do not like each other. As a result, the various family members do not manifest their own unique qualities and characteristics. This restrictive coding rule inhibits the family group's emotional and intellectual growth. Opportunities for expression are narrowly defined and a member's individual qualities are not used to provide an enriching experience for all.

It's Best to Hint Around

In the it's best to hint around family communication rule, the various family group members refuse to explicitly state their case or ask for what they want due to their expectation and/or fear of rejection. Such rejection insulation takes the form of self statements such as, "Although I didn't get my way, the other members still care about me since after all, they really didn't understand my needs." Hinting around allows the individual to avoid taking a stand and gives him or her an emotional out when the results are less than he desires. On the other hand, this rule also assures that the relationship outcome is seldom what the family members desire.

The Generalizing General Rule

In the generalizing general rule, the various family members consistently overstate the reality of the particular moment or event. Such expansive statements lead to arguments about the generalization rather than a discussion about what the relationship members want from each other in the here and now. For example:

HUSBAND:
> You never take the initiative in our sex life. You never take the aggressive part.

WIFE:
> That's not true. Just last week . . . [*Couple argues indefinitely.*]

In this illustration, the husband's generalization (i.e., "never") did not lead to a discussion of what he wanted from his wife at that particular moment. The wife picked up on the "never," felt criticized, and proceded to argue her case. Both the husband and the wife then became involved in a long-term game of "I'm right and you're wrong," rather than trying to find ways of being close that are satisfying to both.

HOW FAMILY MEMBERS HEAR WHAT HAS BEEN SAID TO WHOM (FAMILY DECODING OPERATIONS)

The question, "How are the family members hearing what has been said to whom?" refers to the family's rules about family communication decoding operations. Families and their individual members also tend to develop patterns and rules about how they hear and evaluate the messages they receive from others (Satir, 1964; Lantz, 1975). Such patterns of hearing and evaluating are functional when they are in tune with the objective reality of the particular situation, are life preserving, and help the family members decrease personal and interpersonal conflict (Maultsby, 1975). It is important that the family members develop patterns of accurate communication decoding operations, as many of our emotions are caused by the cognitive evaluations that we make about our environment, self, situation, and others (Lantz, 1975). There are a number of dysfunctional decoding rules that are found in family groups that tend to result in the family members experiencing excessive difficulty in their family life. Such dysfunctional family decoding rules include (1) labeling; (2) blame is the game; (3) it's all my fault; (4) a difference is dangerous; and (5) you're doing what I want isn't what I want.

Labeling

In the labeling decoding operation, the family membership uses the technique of irrational labeling to explain each other's behavior. For example, a divorced mother who labels her son as being "just like your no-good father," may be using the labeling method as a way to decrease her own feelings of inadequacy or guilt. The label acts as a way of explaining a particular behavior, but inhibits effective problem solving. If the son is really just like his no-good father (i.e., it's in the genes), why bother trying to develop a different relationship outcome? Another difficulty with the labeling operation is that it often stimulates the same behavior that the labeler is trying to explain or is concerned about. In addition, a dysfunctional pattern of labeling (labeling that does not reflect the objective reality) tends to facilitate distance between the various family members since it does not allow them to experience or receive each other's full range of human uniqueness.

Blame Is the Game

Many family groups develop the cognitive decoding habit of blaming each other for their own feelings and behavior. This mutual rule of responsibility projection (i.e., it's all your fault) serves the function of decreasing personal pain at the expense of others, and allows each family member to wait for the other members to change. Such cognitive decoding rules inhibit family communication, since after all, if it's all your fault, there is no reason for me to talk about anything. Such family projection often results in a family scapegoat, identified patient or person in pain, whom the family group takes to an agency for a "magic cure."

It's All My Fault

In many family groups, various family members evaluate all family difficulties as being "all my fault." Such dysfunctional responsibility grabbing often reflects a desire for attention that is either not being heard by the other family members, or is being communicated to the other members in an incongruent way. Such dysfunctional responsibility grabbing seldom results in mutual relationship outcomes and can often be used by the problem grabber as a method of controlling others (i.e., I'm such a slob—please pity me). It also tends to provoke distance, since a depressed martyr is seldom all that much fun.

A Difference Is Dangerous

In the "a difference is dangerous" family decoding communication rule, the family members tend to evaluate each others differentness as being an assault on their own personhood. Differentness in others is

interpreted as a critical statement about self. Family groups that oper-
ate under this type of decoding rule tend to develop rigid stereotyped
patterns of relating. Outsiders (such as family therapists) are often
struck by the contrast of verbal togetherness and emotional distance
that is exhibited in this type of family group. The difference is dangerous decoding operation also leads to a decrease in family growth and
functions as a way of preventing the family members full expression of
their own unique individuality.

Your Doing What I Want Isn't What I Want

In the "your doing what I want isn't what I want" family decoding
operation, the family members have learned to ask other family members to behave in a certain way and then evaluate that behavior as not
being "what I want." For example:

FATHER:
   Come here and give me a hug.

[*Son hugs his father.*]

[*Father stiffens up.*]

   In this illustration, the father asked the son for a hug, evaluated
the hug as being "not what I want," and then, by stiffening up, sent the
son a negative nonverbal message. This process has been described in
family literature under the heading of double binds (Bateson, 1958).
This type of decoding (which then results in an incongruent coding
operation) can leave other family members in a position where they are
confused and may not be able to achieve their relationship goals no
matter what they do. This process insures that the family members are
unable to meet their needs for sense and order, and in some instances,
may lead to the development of a schizophrenic family member (Glick
and Kessler, 1974; Haley, 1967; Laing, 1965).

FAMILY ASSESSMENT GUIDELINES AND PROCEDURES

Family assessment is not a totally objective process. It includes the
therapist's subjective experience of being with the family group in the
family group interview. This "being with" includes the therapist's observations and reactions to the family's various transactional patterns
that occur during the family interview. The therapist is less concerned

with what the family members may say about their life outside of the interview situation than how they relate to each other and the therapist during the interview. The time and space of the family group interview can be viewed as a canvas upon which the family group will paint a transactional picture that is fairly illustrative of the general family life. Such a canvas is not entirely empty, as it does include the therapist's attitudes, feelings, and behavior. However, if the therapist is sufficiently aware of his or her own transactional operations, he can still make significant assessment use of this "family painting." Even though the experienced family therapist can be remarkably accurate in his or her subjective judgment, it is often helpful to use certain structured assessment procedures. Three such useful procedures are the following: (1) the plan a picnic procedure; (2) the projective procedure; and (3) the marbles test procedure.

The Plan a Picnic Procedure

The plan a picnic procedure was, to my knowledge, originally developed by Watzlawick (1966) as part of his structured family interview. In the plan a picnic procedure, the therapist asks the family as a group to plan a family outing such as a picnic. The therapist then bows out of the interaction and watches the family members attempt to accomplish the task through their functioning as a group. This procedure can help highlight various patterns of dysfunctional coding and decoding operations as well as the family group's transactional flow. When using this procedure (as well as the other two procedures), the therapist attempts to observe how the various family members (1) manifest self to others; (2) allow others to manifest self to them; and (3) negotiate for mutual outcomes (Andrews, 1974).

The Projective Procedure

In the projective procedure, the family therapist presents the family with an ambiguous stimuli such as a Rorschach or T.A.T. card and then asks the family to decide what the card looks like or means to them as a group (Glick and Kessler, 1974). This task, which almost always insures some different opinions, allows the therapist to observe how the family members function in a decision-making situation. Again, dysfunctional, as well as functional, transactional processes are highlighted for the therapist in the family group interview (Glick and Kessler, 1974).

The Marbles Test Procedure

The marbles test has been reported by Bodin and Farber (1973). In the marbles test, the therapist asks the family members to make something together out of a group of marbles and a square board that has holes in it in which one can place the marbles. The number of holes and the variety and number of marbles depends upon the size of the family group. The task again allows the therapist the opportunity to observe family group transactions without a great deal of therapeutic contamination. This task, with its wide variety of possibilities and alternatives, gives the family ample opportunity to demonstrate its various communication rules, power alignments, and decision-making processes.

DEVELOPING A TREATMENT CONTRACT

In recent years a number of family therapists have stressed the need to develop a treatment contract in the initial stage of family therapy (Haley, 1976; Minuchin, 1974). Developing a treatment contract is important as it helps both the family therapist and the family group have a set of goals, a sense of direction, and a way for each therapy participant to meet their needs for sense-order and production. Without a treatment contract, neither the family nor the therapist will know what to expect or the direction of the therapy process.

The author's approach to developing a treatment contract is somewhat different from what is usually suggested and is based upon the assumption that the contract should be developed only after the family group has been able to produce a small interactional change during the initial family interview. If such a change does not occur, the treatment contract should call only for further assessment.

Very often in the initial family interview, the family group will attempt to pressure the therapist into a premature contract that may include goals and expectations that will hinder the family therapy process.

For example, in the initial contact with the Kerb family, Mr. and Mrs. Kerb both agreed that their purpose in attending family therapy was to obtain either hospitalization or medication for their oldest daughter Susan. They stated that Susan was the only problem in the family. These verbal statements were not congruent with the couple's nonverbal behavior during the interview. The daughter sat between Mr. and Mrs. Kerb and most messages between the parents were channeled through the daughter. This process was interrupted by the family therapist who suggested that the parents check out with each other if their various assumptions were correct. This interactional change resulted in a confession by both the husband and the wife that they were in fact having trouble getting along and that most of their time together was being spent trying to figure out "what to do about Susan." In this family, the daughter's "problems" served as a sort of cement for the parents' marriage. The treatment contract between the therapist and the family was developed after the parents expressed a desire to "improve our relationship" as well as "help Susan." The family and therapist contracted for ten family therapy sessions to explore and improve family communication.

In this illustration, the treatment contract was developed after the initial assessment and after the family made a small interactional change. This helped the family experience the benefits of a family interactional change and the family was able to accept a treatment contract that would have been resisted if negotiated at first. The daughter remained out of the hospital, did not need medication, and the parents were able to improve their relationship.

SUMMARY

The initial stage of family group therapy includes: (1) developing a therapeutic alliance, (2) making a family transactional assessment, and (3) developing a treatment contract. The process of developing a therapeutic alliance includes the elements and procedures of structure, emotional accommodation, the acceptance of symptoms, and the various mimicking behaviors of the family therapist. In the assessment process, the therapist pays attention to the family rules about coding operations, decoding operations, the family's transactional flow, and also how the family members go about the process of negotiating for a joint relationship outcome. Developing a treatment contract follows assessment, relationship building and the instigation of a small family interactional change. After this initial stage the family therapist turns his or her attention primarily toward intervention. Family therapy intervention can be viewed as a family group transactional reshaping process. This reshaping process will be examined in Chapter Three.

3

Family Therapy Intervention

The goal of the family therapist is to help the family group interrupt, challenge, and change those dysfunctional, repetitive family group transactions that inhibit the family membership from meeting their individual psychological needs (Lantz, 1977). Such a transactional reshaping process includes change in the family group structure, coding operations, and decoding operations. The therapist attempts to induce change by promoting functional communication. Such functional family communication can result from a therapeutic process in which the therapist helps the family membership (1) manifest themselves clearly to others; (2) allow others to manifest themselves clearly; and (3) then negotiate with each other for joint relationship outcomes (Andrews, 1974; Satir, 1965). The therapist attempts to induce this therapeutic process through the use of a variety of interventive strategies. Such interventive strategies can include the following: (1) clarification of communication; (2) redirecting communication; (3) relabeling; (4) modeling; (5) therapeutic binds; (6) provocative exagger-

Sections of this chapter appeared in "Family Therapy: Using a Transactional Approach." *Journal of Psychiatric Nursing* (15)4:17–22, April 1977, and are reprinted with the permission of Margaret Carnine, R.N., Managing Editor.

ation; (7) forcing congruent expression of self; (8) boundary setting; (9) homework; (10) the development of insight; and (11) environmental manipulation (Lantz, 1977).

CLARIFICATION OF COMMUNICATION

Clarification of communication is an intervention strategy in which the therapist places himself in the role of a middleman. In this middleman role, the therapist interrupts the relationship members' transactional process and then takes on the function of clarifying the members' dysfunctional coding and decoding operations. For example:

HUSBAND:

But, I get so damn mad. Like, I get home from work real tired, you know, and the first thing that happens is she hits me in the face with all the things I'm supposed to do—punish the kids, fix this or that, so, after a while, you know, I get mad and let her have it.

(Husband communicates his frustration and anger, but not his desire for support.)

WIFE:

He just doesn't show any interest in the house or the kids.

(Wife doesn't mention that she wants his interest.)

HUSBAND:

The hell I don't! If I wasn't interested, you don't think I'd be out working my ass off, do you?

(Husband defends against the attack he perceives his wife is making.)

THERAPIST:

I'm hearing you both say the same thing. It's like you both want some appreciation from each other. You've both been working all day and you're tired and when you meet each other, you're both wanting something from each other. But, what it is doesn't seem to get across. Like do you hear your wife saying she wants some attention from you?

(Therapist injects himself into the transactions to point out the underlying message both husband and wife are *not saying*.)

HUSBAND:

No.

THERAPIST:
> That's what I hear.

> (Therapist checks out with the couple whether or not he was getting their real meaning.)

[*Silence*]

THERAPIST:
> Do you hear your husband saying he wants some attention or appreciation?

WIFE:
> No.

THERAPIST:
> That's what I hear.

[*Silence*]

HUSBAND:
> Yea. Well, there's probably something to that.

THERAPIST:
> So, I'm hearing you right, that correct?

HUSBAND:
> Yea.

> (Husband agrees that this is the underlying message.)

THERAPIST:
> What about you? Am I hearing you right?

In this illustration, the therapist injected himself into the couple's transactional exchange. The therapist took the distorted messages and evaluations that were being made, and sent, clarified, to the couple what he was hearing in the distorted transactions, and then checked out with the relationship pair whether or not his evaluation was correct. Such a process can be illustrated as in Figure 8.

Figure 8.   *The therapist as a middle person*

This process of clarification is an educational process in the sense that the relationship members can use it in a way that allows them to see the large discrepancies between (1) what they are saying and what others are hearing; (2) what they are hearing and what others are saying; and (3) what both self and others mean, but are not saying in a clear, congruent way. Initially, the therapist will be very active in his or her use of the clarification process. However, as time goes on and the family members develop an awareness of the types and extent of their distorted communication patterns, the relationship members will begin to start clarifying for themselves. When this begins to occur, the therapist will decrease the frequency of his clarification and middle-man role.

REDIRECTING COMMUNICATION

Many family groups come to the family therapist with a learned pattern of indirect communication. Examples of indirect communication patterns include (1) a husband who expresses hostility to his wife through one of the children; (2) a wife who confides to her mother-in-law in the hopes that the mother-in-law will say something that will "shape up" the wife's husband; and (3) a child who tells his father that "mother said it was okay" in the hopes of getting permission from one parent, knowing full well that the other parent has already said no. Families that exhibit this type of indirect communication will tend to try and talk to the therapist rather then to each other during the family group interview. The therapist can counter this process by (1) structuring the therapy in a way that forces the family members to interact directly and (2) by stubbornly insisting that the family members ask and tell one another. The following segment illustrates a number of ways in which the therapist can redirect family communication.

THERAPIST:

Okay, what I'd like you to do today is to take a few minutes and think about what concerns you have and who in the family you want to talk to about those concerns.

(Therapist structures the situation.)

MOTHER:

[*Talking to the therapist*] Well, I'm upset about Johnny. All he ever does is act like a smart aleck.

(Mother talks about son rather than to the son.)

THERAPIST:

So, you've got a concern with Johnny. Do

(Therapist points out

you have any objections about talking to him about it?

MOTHER:

Well, he never listens.

THERAPIST:

Talk to him about it. Ask him if he'd be willing to listen. Turn your chair around and look at him.

MOTHER:

I don't know where to start.

THERAPIST:

So, tell him you don't know where to start.

MOTHER:

[Looking at son] I don't like it when you don't listen.

(again what he wants the family to do.)

(Therapist points out interactional alternatives.)

(Therapist gives the client a place to start.)

(Client responds by sending a clear message to her son.)

In this illustration, the therapist provided the family with an expectation (i.e., talk to each other) and then actively and directly insisted that the family members meet that expectation. The therapist's expectation was a result of his assessment of the family interactional style and his opinion that the family could make good use of a different kind of transactional experience during the family group interview.

Many families respond to such an approach by increasing the number of times they communicate to each other in a direct way. It is often found that when the therapist provokes a small number of direct transactions between family members during the family group interview, the family takes this experience with them and will then increase its production of direct transactions outside of the therapy situation. This occurs because such direct family communication is rewarding due to the fact that it increases the family's chances of meeting its members' psychological needs. As a result, the family members often feel better and then tend to increase those types of behaviors that have resulted in a more favorable relationship outcome.

RELABELING

As Ellis (1962) and Tosi (1974) have noted, many of our feelings are a direct result of the beliefs and evaluations we have and make about ourself and our social situation. Families often share a set of cognitive beliefs, evaluations, and communication rules that must be countered by the therapist if the family is to increase its capacity for healthy human growth (Zuk, 1972). One strategy for countering dysfunctional family myths is the process of therapeutic relabeling. Therapeutic relabeling is a process in which the family therapist suggests a new or different evaluation of a given phenomenon to the members of the family group, which will result in a more positive interactional outcome (Zuk, 1972). For example:

WIFE:
> [*Angry tone*] I get sick of your excuses and reasons.

HUSBAND:
> [*Glaring at wife*] Excuses hell. If you'd stop nagging long enough to listen, maybe I could explain.

WIFE:
> [*To therapist*] What are you laughing about?

THERAPIST:
> I'm just really happy that the two of you care enough to have these fights. I get worried when couples don't have the courage to fight it out.

In this illustration, the therapist relabeled and reevaluated the couple's fight as having some positive qualities. The therapist pointed out that the fight was evidence that the couple had positive feelings about each other. Such a new evaluation then often leads to a change in the family's interactional process, which in turn "feels better" and will then tend to be repeated in the family's day-to-day living.

Relabeling can occur in two distinct ways. It can occur as a result of the therapist using his or her "expert authority role" to influence the family's perception of a given set of family behaviors, or it can occur as a result of the therapist setting up an experiental situation which results in the family doing the relabeling for themselves (Haley, 1963).

MODELING

Many families come to the therapist never having learned specific, functional communication skills. Such a family group has been described as a closed system (Satir, 1964). With this type of family it is often valuable for the therapist to act as a communication model. In this role, the therapist exhibits what was discussed in Chapter 1 and has been labeled by Satir (1964) as "maturation." When the therapist is able to act out a maturation transactional style, i.e., (1) he is fully in charge of himself; (2) he makes accurate perceptions; (3) he owns those perceptions as being his own; and (4) he makes rational decisions based on those perceptions, he is putting into operation what has been called an open system (Andrews, 1974). When operating as an open communication system, the therapist feels free to comment on or talk about anything he or she thinks, feels, sees, or does not understand (Andrews, 1974). By doing this, the therapist is providing for the family group, a method and style of functional communicating which gives the family group alternative ways of relating. Such modeling is important as it provides specific communication skills rather than simply talking about what might be possible.

Modeling can become an even more powerful interventive strategy when exhibited by a co-therapy team. Co-therapists, like any other fallible human beings, have differences, disagreements, and unique individualized goals. Such differences are a fact of life and cannot be successfully ignored. However, if the co-therapists practice what they preach and are willing to manifest themselves clearly to each other, listen to each other, and then negotiate for mutual outcomes, they can provide an extremely useful and powerful experiential model for the family group membership.

Providing such a communication model for the disturbed family group sets up a conflict situation. In this conflict situation, an open system (the therapist or co-therapist team) comes into interaction with a closed system (the disturbed family group). The open system will attempt to change the closed system's communication rules, and the closed system will attempt to change the open system's communication rules. This conflict situation can be illustrated as in Figure 9, which is an adaptation of a model presented by Andrews (1974).

In this conflict situation, one of three things can occur. First, the family can teach the therapist to be a closed system. This process is often occuring when (1) the therapist begins to reschedule the family group's meetings due to an excessive number of other meetings that the therapist "must" attend; (2) the therapist develops somatic complaints just prior to the family group interview; and (3) the therapist makes

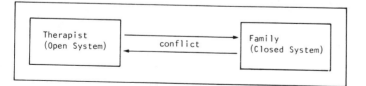

Figure 9.   *The therapy conflict situation (Adapted from Andrews, 1974)*

poorly thought out rationales that indicate that a particular family member needs hospitalization, medications, individual therapy, group therapy, or any other treatment modality that the family therapist doesn't provide.

Secondly, the therapist can teach the family to be an open communication system. This occurs when the family members (1) begin to talk to each other rather than about each other; (2) start using "I" statements; and (3) begin to give up their depression, anxiety, and/or somatic complaints.

A final option is for the therapist and family to terminate their relationship. This third option often occurs when the family group is in conflict with a third party such as the court, police, or a protective service agency. In these instances, the family group often views the therapy process as a way of getting the referral agency "off our backs." In such instances, the family may get caught up into the therapy process even though their initial motivation was hardly what the therapist would desire. In some instances, the family will change because the therapist will openly threaten termination unless they change. When this occurs, the family will generally offer the least amount of change they feel will be accepted by the family therapist. In these situations, the therapist can often get the family involved by demanding a large change. If the family changes to keep the therapist involved and the referring agency off their backs, they may experience that change as beneficial. When this occurs, the family may renegotiate for further change. In spite of the many options for therapeutic involvement, some family groups simply do not wish to change or cannot be helped by a particular therapist. In such instances, it is often wise to accept the inevitable. The family may return at a later date.

THERAPEUTIC BINDS

As was noted in Chapter Two, many family groups are frightened of change. The family group comes to the family therapist with a transactional style that has been learned through repetition over a long period of time. Although this learned transactional style may not be functional in terms of meeting the family members' psychological needs, it is a comfortable style in the sense that it is known and familiar to the family membership. Change implies risk. As a result, every family group will to some degree resist and avoid the anxiety implied in new behaviors and family change. Such family resistance (resistance by the system as a whole) is to be expected by the family therapist and can be used as an indication that the therapist is headed in the right direction. Without some resistance, it can be assumed that not much different is happening in or out of the family sessions.

Even though family resistance is to be expected and can be viewed as an indicator of therapeutic movement, it sometimes can become a major stumbling block to successful family therapy. In many instances, such family resistance can be handled through reassurance, emotional accommodation, and support. However, when such methods are not sufficient, the therapist may need to resort to a therapeutic bind (Haley, 1976).

A therapeutic bind is a manuever in which the family therapist prescribes either the family's resistance or the symptoms found within the family group (Haley, 1963). This manuever places the therapist in a position of power and control. Since the therapist has prescribed the symptom and/or resistance, the family group can no longer use the prescribed behavior as a way of avoiding therapeutic interaction. The family is put into the position of either (1) continuing the behavior (which is doing what the therapist asks and sets the norm that the family will act out other prescribed behaviors—even functional ones) or (2) changing the dysfunctional behavior into a more healthy family interaction. Therapeutic binds can be directed toward behaviors that occur within the family group interview or toward behaviors that occur outside of the family group interview. The following vignettes illustrate a number of ways in which the family therapist can make constructive use of the therapeutic bind.

Mr. and Mrs. Baldwin

Mr. and Mrs. Baldwin were referred for conjoint marital therapy by their family physician. The Baldwins had gone to their family doctor due to "Mr. Baldwin's impotence," which first started approximately seven months prior to the initial marital interview. At that time, Mr. Baldwin had attempted intercourse with his wife on their anniversary, On that evening, Mr. Baldwin was unable to "perform," felt guilty, and his wife became angry. In subsequent weeks, Mr. Baldwin felt worried and depressed. Mrs. Baldwin was angry as she interpreted the problem as a rejection of her. This set up the reciprocal cycle of a depressed husband, an angry wife, and a mutual agreement by the marital pair to avoid each other and the problem.

Therapeutic intervention centered around prescribing the impotence symptom. Mr. and Mrs. Baldwin were instructed to spend two hours per evening for two weeks together in bed "naked and necking." They were told that under no circumstances were they allowed to engage in sexual intercourse. It was stressed that such an abstinence was necessary to the treatment plan.

Two weeks later, the couple enthusiastically reported that they were "bad," had not followed the therapist's instructions, and had spent most of their evenings together engaging in sexual intercourse. In this instance, the therapeutic bind allowed the couple to interact without guilt and anger, had taken off the pressure to perform, and allowed nature to run its course.

Mr. and Mrs. Montroy

Mr. and Mrs. Montroy were referred for conjoint marital therapy by their attorney. Within the marital sessions, the couple exhibited a mutually antagonistic interactional style (attack-attack) which included projection, blame, labeling, and hostile verbal assaults. Both Mr. and Mrs. Montroy were able to manifest anger but neither individual could express their underlying feelings of depression and loneliness. After a number of attempts to get the couple to express those underlying feelings, the therapist used a therapeutic bind. During the fourth session, the therapist commented that the couple really did seem to want to make use of the therapy hour for fighting. The therapist suggested that the couple increase the fighting and "really get into it" by hitting each other with pillows. This intervention led to an opposite type of resistance which in turn resulted in the couple finally expressing to each other their mutual sadness and desire for support.

PROVOCATIVE EXAGGERATION

Provocative exaggeration is a strategy in which the therapist uses humor, exaggeration, and absurd statements to help the family group members change distorted coding and decoding operations (Farrelly and Brandsma, 1974).

For example, in the Haney family, Mrs. Haney used responsibility grabbing and a "if it weren't for me" transactional style to control her family through the encouragement of guilt. Mr. Haney and the children reinforced the process by playing "nice guy" and getting back at Mrs. Haney through the use of subtle back-stabbing measures that could easily be denied. As a result, Mrs. Haney felt more alone, which exacerbated the process. Therapeutic intervention was initially focused upon helping the family members directly express their wants, desires, and resentments. Mrs. Haney helped the family maintain the status quo through the use of timely, guilt-producing depressions whenever she was asked to change. In the following segment, the therapist confronts Mrs. Haney and her irrational decoding operations through the use of provocative exaggeration:

MR. HANEY:
> Well, I get good and mad when you don't do what you say you're going to do.

MRS. HANEY:
> [*Depressed tone, looking towards therapist*] See look what I've done. I've destroyed my husband's life.

THERAPIST:
> [*Exaggerated concern*] You wouldn't do that to me, would you?

MRS. HANEY:
> [*Smiles*]

THERAPIST:
> After all, I'm in the prime of my life. I don't want to take any chances on being destroyed. Maybe I should hide. [*Therapist moves and hides behind the curtains in the office.*]

MR. AND MRS. HANEY:
> [*Both are laughing*]

THERAPIST:
> [*Quivering*] Please, Mrs. Haney, don't destroy my life.

MRS. HANEY:
> [*Laughing*] Okay, enough. So I haven't destroyed his life.

THERAPIST:
> [*Confused*] You mean you was telling a fib?

MRS. HANEY:
> [*Laughing*] Yes, I told a fib.

THERAPIST:
> [*Also laughing*] What a relief.

Provocative exaggeration can be an extremely effective way of challenging distorted messages and dysfunctional transactions. Like any other powerful tool, it is equally dangerous and should not be used unless the therapist is confident that he has a solid relationship with all members of the family group. The method is not to be used by the therapist as a way to get back at the family if the therapist is angry.

FORCING CONGRUENT EXPRESSION OF SELF

Many families come to the therapist with a well-practiced interactional pattern of mutual isolation, avoidance, and incongruent communication. The family members seem welded to their isolation and are extremely resistant to making contact. In this type of family, the members do not really know each other. Most of the family members, for a variety of reasons, have not manifested themselves to the other members in a clear, precise, congruent way. This type of family interaction leads to tremendous decoding distortions, as none of the members are presented with an explicit verbal reality base that would allow them the opportunity to check out their cognitive evaluations. In some instances hallucinations and delusions may develop. In this type of family, the therapist's goal is to facilitate direct and congruent interaction. The therapist facilitates such congruent interaction by acting as an "instigator." Such an instigator role includes the use of support, structure, provocative statements, and experiential exercises. For example:

THERAPIST:
Okay, what I want you to do is turn your chairs toward each other and tell each other the first thing that comes to your mind.

(Therapist structures the situation. Moving chairs and having family members look at each other is an experiential way of setting a talking, contact norm.)

[Family moves chairs]

[Silence]

WIFE:
[Meekly] I don't know where to start.

[Husband is looking at the walls in the therapist's office.]

THERAPIST:
Tell your husband that you're better looking than the walls.

(Therapist uses humor to provoke husband.)

[Husband laughs.]

WIFE:
[Forcefully] I'm better looking than the walls.

THERAPIST:

> That's a good start. Try it a bit louder. You know, with a little more feeling.
>
> (Therapist supports wife's effort at involvement.)

In the instigator role, the therapist is using a practice that Ackerman has labeled as "tickling the defenses" (Ackerman, 1966). In this role, the therapist manifests himself as an alive human being who is willing to be involved and expects such involvement from the family group. The therapist offers an experience in living. Such a confrontive experience, coupled with the necessary support, may facilitate within the family system a feeling of hope, excitement, and the belief that a different way of relating is imminently possible.

BOUNDARY SETTING

As noted in Chapters One and Two, many family groups develop a transaction style that includes inappropriate involvement of the children in the parents' marital realtionship. Boundary setting is an attempt by the family therapist to decrease the family group's tendency to violate generational boundaries. Boundary setting can occur within the family group interview, but also can result from specific task assignments prescribed by the therapist that the family group is to accomplish at home. The following vignette illustrates both types of boundary setting.

The Harper family was referred for family therapy by their son's school counselor. The school counselor was concerned with the son's poor attendance, temper outbursts, and marginal grades. After a conference with the parents, the school counselor referred the family for therapy because of her suspicion that something was amiss in the functioning of the family as a group. The family membership included Roger (14-year-old son), Jane (11-year-old daughter), Mr. Harper (45-year-old father), and Mrs. Harper (43-year-old mother). The family seating arrangement in the first interview is illustrated in Figure 10.

In the initial interview, Roger would act up (i.e., flick cigarette ashes on the floor), mother would tell him to stop, Roger would talk back, father would grin, and mother would become silent. Jane acted as an isolate as all this was going on. This process was repeated in various forms during the first half of the initial interview. The therapist viewed the repetitive process as an excellent example of the minor as parental conflict weapon syndrome and decided to intervene through the use of boundary setting within the conjoint interview. The bound-

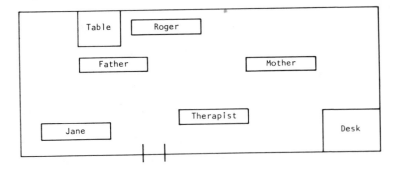

Figure 10. *The Harper family*

ary setting occurred by helping the wife ask the husband for support as a way of breaking up the dysfunctional, repetitive process. For example:

[Son flicking ashes on the floor.]

MOTHER:
　　[Meekly] Roger, stop that. That's no way
　　to act.

SON:
　　[Angry] Get off my back.

FATHER:
　　[Silent]　　　　　　　　　　　　　(No support)

THERAPIST:
　　You know, it looks to me like you need　(Suggests that wife and
　　some help right now but you're not asking　husband work together)
　　your husband.

MOTHER:
　　[Silent . . . tearing]　　　　　　　(Tells the therapist he is
　　　　　　　　　　　　　　　　　　　on the right track)

THERAPIST:
　　Do I see some tears?

MOTHER:
　　[Crying]

THERAPIST:
　　What's it about?

MOTHER:
　　Nothing.

THERAPIST:
　　You afraid he won't help?　　　　　　(Clarifies)

MOTHER:
> [*Nods yes.*]

THERAPIST:
> Let's find out. Ask him for some help.   (Reinforces her for wanting help)

WIFE:
> [*Looks toward husband*]

THERAPIST:
> [*To husband*] Well, what about it. You   (Supports wife's attempt)
> want to give her some help?

HUSBAND:
> Well, I always try to be available to her   (Intellectualizes)
> when I can. I'm gone a lot working.

THERAPIST:
> Sometimes you're far away?   (Points out the issue)

HUSBAND:
> Yea.

THERAPIST:
> You far away right now?

HUSBAND:
> [*Softly*] No.   (Husband may be willing to help wife.)

THERAPIST:
> It's too bad you're sitting far away from   (Points out incongruence)
> her when you don't feel far away.

HUSBAND:
> [*Beginning to tear up*] I'm not always sure   (Husband presents his fear.)
> she wants me.

THERAPIST:
> When she looked at you, you weren't sure
> what she meant?

HUSBAND:
> Well, I'm not always sure.

THERAPIST:
> Ask her if she wants you far away.   (Tells husband to check it out)

HUSBAND:
> Do you?

WIFE:
> No.

THERAPIST:
> You might start by sitting next to her.   (Suggests alternative)

HUSBAND
    [Changes chairs and holds wife's hand.]
THERAPIST:
    [To wife] Does that feel better?   (Reinforces generational
                                                          boundary)

WIFE:
    [Smiles]
THERAPIST:
    [To husband] You feel comfortable?
HUSBAND:
    Yea.
THERAPIST:
    It looks a lot better this way. It looked kind   (Reinforces generational
    of confusing to me when you were sitting   boundary)
    apart. Do you sit together much at home?
HUSBAND:
    No.
THERAPIST:
    That might be something to work on.   (Sets the stage for a con-
                                                          tract and a task assign-
                                                          ment)

After this exchange (which illustrated to the therapist that both parents were open to improving their relationship), the therapist followed up by asking the marital couple to spend two hours per week together doing things without the children. This task assignment reinforced the boundary that had been initially set within the conjoint interview.

HOMEWORK

Homework can be viewed as a task assignment used by the family therapist to extend, reinforce, and promote those changed family behaviors that occur within the family interview to the family's outside daily life. Homework can be geared toward boundary setting, coding operations, and decoding operations. It can be used to help strengthen a family subsystem (i.e., the marital pair) or to help family members practice and develop specific communication skills. Examples of homework would include having family members spend a prescribed amount of time together, assigning specific family group activities, having the family members read certain books, having the family members listen to tape recordings of their own interviews, having the family members keep a diary, and having the family members practice relationship skills through the use of various structured group activities. The creative use of homework assignments is limited only by the therapist's imagination and understanding of family group dynamics.

THE DEVELOPMENT OF INSIGHT

Very often the disturbed family group is unaware of those dysfunctional repetitive group processes that inhibit them from meeting their psychological needs. What is often viewed by clinicians as resistance may in fact be a lack of information. As a result it is often advisable to help the family group become more aware of what they are doing as a system that isn't working out. If this is the case, helping the family group generate new information can become an important part of the therapeutic task. The therapist can help the family group generate such new information through the use of feedback mechanisms such as (1) bringing symptoms alive in the interview; (2) sculpting; and (3) the use of recording equipment.

Bringing Symptoms Alive in the Interview

The following case vignette illustrates one way in which the therapist can help the family gain new information by bringing symptoms alive in the interview situation.

MOTHER:
  [To therapist] It starts when it's time to get up and go to school. He won't get up.
THERAPIST:
  Okay. I really want to understand how that goes. Let's role play it right now. Okay, where's Johnny?
FATHER:
  In bed.
THERAPIST:
  Okay, so where are you?
MOTHER:
  I'm fixing breakfast and he's at the table.

THERAPIST:
> So, Johnny's in bed. You're fixing breakfast and Dad's at the table. So then what happened?

MOTHER:
> Nothing. He doesn't come down.

THERAPIST:
> Well, do you ask him to?

MOTHER:
> Yea.

THERAPIST:
> Well, show me. Okay, Dad, this is the table. You sit at the table and this is the stove. You stand at the stove. Johnny, you just sit where you are and do just like you do in the mornings. Okay, now show me what happens next.

MOTHER:
> Well, I . . .

THERAPIST:
> No. Show me. Do it. Just like it happens at home.

Through this role play situation, the family was able to show the therapist exactly what they "do" in the mornings. The process was brought alive in the interview. It became clear that the parents did not work together in training the son to get up on time. As a result, both felt frustrated, got mad at each other, and mother finally ended up screaming at the child. The child then took his upset feelings out on the other school children which resulted in the school sending him home for the day. As a result of this role play situation, the parents were able to get a better idea of what they were doing that didn't work. This resulted in some experimentation that helped the family group develop more functional patterns at the beginning of their day.

Sculpting

Sculpting is a process which the therapist can use to help the family members check out with each other how each individual member understands, views, and feels about the total family group system. In this process, the therapist asks each family member to build a statue that represents to the individual how the family operates as a group. The individual is asked to use the interview room, himself, and the other family members as sculpting material (Simon, 1972).

After each family member has built a family statue, the family as a group is asked to discuss with each other what they have learned about themselves, each other, and the functioning of the total family group. This process often results in some excellent problem solving by the family members. It facilitates manifestation of self and negotiation for joint relationship outcomes.

The Use of Recording Equipment

The family therapist can make excellent use of audio and audiovisual equipment when attempting to help the family group generate new information. Family members are often quite amazed when presented with the opportunity to see and hear themselves interacting with the other family members.

For example, Mrs. Alex requested family therapy because her two teen-age daughters were acting rebellious. Mrs. Alex stated that her daughters were coming home past curfew, talking back, and very often refused to listen. During the family group interview, Mrs. Alex and the children whined, shouted, blamed, and in the therapist's opinion, verbally abused each other. The daughters felt mother was verbally abusive, Mrs. Alex felt the daughters were verbally abusive, but no one in the family agreed with the therapist that, "they all sounded like a herd of trumpeting, thundering elephants." The family was quite shocked to hear themselves shouting so loud when the therapist played back the recorded interview. All family members then contracted to tone it down. This was the first step toward mutual understanding for each family member's unique individual needs.

ENVIRONMENTAL MANIPULATION

It has long been recognized that environmental stress can exacerbate any family's tendency toward dysfunctional behavior. Families, as well as individuals, are a part of a larger context. As a part of that context, all families are influenced and affected by environmental stress. The effective family clinician remembers this fact and is willing to provide information, concrete services, referral, and in many instances, will act as an advocate for the family group. The active use of social services such as financial aid, housing programs, job training, job placement, day care, homemakers, and the Big Brother Organization can be an effective way to decrease family stress.

SUMMARY

The author has presented a number of methods and procedures that can be used by the family therapist in his or her attempt to help the family group change those dysfunctional family processes that inhibit the family members from meeting their psychological needs. The following three chapters will illustrate these methods by presenting family interview vignettes. The first two illustrations (Chapters Four and Five) will present segments where the therapist is working with a marital couple. Working with the dyad is the simplest form of conjoint therapy and can also be viewed as the easiest way to illustrate the numerous processes that occur in conjoint interviewing. Chapter Six will present an illustration in which the therapist is working with the total family group.

4

Mr. and Mrs. Smith: Avoiding Hospitalization

Mr. and Mrs. Smith were referred for conjoint marital therapy after Mr. Smith was released from a state mental hospital. Mr. Smith had been admitted to the hospital twelve times in the last five years. At the time of his last release, Mr. Smith was given the diagnostic label "schizophrenia, paranoid type" and was released on a rather heavy dosage of medication. The hospital staff felt that Mrs. Smith was very much a part of Mr. Smith's "illness" and reported that Mrs. Smith was "overprotective" and "sabotaged hospital efforts aimed at helping Mr. Smith become a more autonomous human being." It was suspected by the hospital staff that Mrs. Smith had in the past asked her husband to stop taking his medication. It was also felt that this precipitated rehospitalization. The posthospitalization treatment plan included (1) conjoint marital therapy, (2) chemotherapy, and (3) the use of social services aimed at decreasing family stress. The marital therapist's approach is geared toward helping the couple send clear messages and making accurate evaluations of the messages they each receive, and toward helping them meet their psychological needs for sense-order and intimacy. The psychological need for sense and order is especially important when working with a family exhibiting a schizophrenic process.

[*Wife comes into the office and closes a
cabinet door that was partially open.*]

HUSBAND:
> You should see her when we go to a
> friend's house.

WIFE:
> They think I'm nuts.

THERAPIST:
> They do?

[*Laughter*]

WIFE:
> I go around shutting their closet doors and
> things.

THERAPIST:
> Yea, I keep forgetting, you have to have
> an immaculate house, right?

WIFE:
> Well . . .

HUSBAND:
> Yes, she does. She tries too hard.

WIFE:
> I like to have it done nice for my hus-
> band.

(Wife does things for her
husband even if he
doesn't want what she
does. Wife does not
check out what the hus-
band wants, yet con-
tinues to insist that she
does it all for him.)

HUSBAND:
> She forgets people live there.

THERAPIST:
> I've talked to John some about this train-
> ing program, and today I would like you
> two to talk to each other about the train-
> ing program and how it will affect both of
> you.

(Therapist has referred
Mr. Smith to a voca-
tional training program.)

WIFE:
> And I'll tell you something else.

THERAPIST:
> What?

WIFE:

It would please me so much if he could get out of the house for three or four hours or even longer, because I want to do something and when he's at the house, I get too nervous when he's there all the time. It's not that I don't want him there.

(Wife sends an unclear message which can easily be distorted by the husband.)

HUSBAND:

Now I get it.

THERAPIST:

Get what?

HUSBAND:

What she's saying.

WIFE:

What I'm saying is that when he was at work and came home I appreciated him more. When he's there constantly . . .

(Wife's coding is not clear, and husband's decoding operation is that his wife does not care about him.)

HUSBAND:

Now she doesn't like me, see . . . I knew it.

WIFE:

No, it ain't that either. I do. But it does get bothersome. You don't feel like doing no work and I don't feel like doing nothing because he's there. I want to be with him all of the time and I can't get none of my stuff done.

(Wife improves her coding operation, but still places the responsibility for her not getting work done on her husband.)

THERAPIST:

How about the two of you turning to each other and talking a little bit about this training and what it's going to mean. I'd like to hear you talk about that. I didn't know how much you've discussed it, but I'd like for you to discuss it some today— the differences and all that. Rather than tell me about it, I'd like the two of you to talk about it with each other.

(The couple have been talking at the therapist. Therapist attempts to redirect the communication process.)

HUSBAND:

I don't know other than to tell her it will be some kind of school.

THERAPIST:
> Tell her.

HUSBAND:
> I'm tellin' her.

THERAPIST:
> You're telling me, John.

(Therapist again states what he wants the couple to do.)

[*Laughter*]

HUSBAND:
> It'd be some kind of school. That's all I got out of it.

WIFE:
> Be like what you had out there at _____?

HUSBAND:
> Yea, it'd be something on that order.

THERAPIST:
> I'd really like the two of you to talk about how the family is going to be affected because it is going to be different, and how is that going to affect you?

HUSBAND:
> It shouldn't make any big changes. I don't do anything around the house anyhow. Just sit there. It shouldn't be any change about that.

WIFE:
> I won't be as disgusted about a lot of things that I am right now. I've been trying to get him to help me clean the garage, which I've done already. I have him to fix the stovepipe, which I can't get him to do. There is several little things. And when he's gone if it's at school or wherever he is, I'm gonna do it myself. If he's there, I won't do it because I want him to.

(The wife often does things for the husband and then complains that he didn't do it.)

(Wife demonstrates a lack of differentiation.)

[*Husband slumps over.*]

(Husband has evaluated wife's message as meaning she doesn't care about him.)

THERAPIST:

What's the matter?

HUSBAND:

Nothing.

WIFE:

That's the matter. That's the way he acts when I talk to him this way.

THERAPIST:

Uh-huh . . .

[Husband laughs]

WIFE:

I'm half afraid to talk to him.

THERAPIST:

You are?

WIFE:

Yea . . . and that goes along with our sex problem, too. If I go over and I put my arms around him, he thinks I want to go to bed with him right away. Isn't true all the time. And, he thinks he's losing his manhood.

(The same process may be occuring in the bedroom.)

THERAPIST:

That's a concern of yours, that he thinks that way?

WIFE:

He told me.

THERAPIST:

Are you worried about his thinking that way?

WIFE:

Of course I'm worried about him thinking that way. He's too young . . . he isn't gonna lose his manhood now. I think it's mostly the pills.

THERAPIST:

That's one of the possible side effects of that medicine.

(Therapist places himself in the middleman role as he realizes there will probably be a good bit of distortion in the couple's communication about this issue.)

WIFE:

And he tells me . . . well, I'll just stop taking the pills and I know if he quits the pills it's gonna make him bad in another way.

[*Silence*]

WIFE:

And it's just a constant bickering between that and I'm half afraid to touch him and kiss him good night or anything because he thinks that is what I want.

THERAPIST:

So you're mad at John because John . . .

WIFE:

No, I ain't mad at him . . . I cry.

THERAPIST:

Well, you're hurt.

WIFE:

Sure.

THERAPIST:

But what are you hurt about?

WIFE:

Because he makes me feel this way.

THERAPIST:

Okay, you're wanting to have some affection and give some affection, and he interprets that as you are coming on sexually.

(Therapist suggests what he thinks is going on about this issue.)

WIFE:

Right.

THERAPIST:

Well, you'd better talk to him about that because he may not understand.

WIFE:

I have.

THERAPIST:

Well talk again. Let me see how you talk about that.

(Therapist attempts to get the couple to talk about this issue with each other after he has clarified the process.)

WIFE:

[*Laughter*] I can't talk to my husband

about the way I feel in front of another
person.

THERAPIST:

You never had any trouble before. I've
heard you yelling at him and all kinds of
stuff, and it didn't bother you.

WIFE:

That's different. I think when two people
are trying to make love or talk about love,
that's for them to hear, not for somebody
else to listen to.

(Wife wants to talk about
the problem rather than
to her husband. This will
insure that the problem
does not get resolved.)

THERAPIST:

We are talking about affection right now.

(Therapist believes that
the couple does not know
how to separate affection
and sex.)

WIFE:

Well affection then, if you want to call it
that. He knows what I mean anyhow .·. .

THERAPIST:

Does he?

WIFE:

Yes.

THERAPIST:

What does she mean?

HUSBAND:

Well, she means I'm too touchy on the
subject, that's all.

THERAPIST:

Touchy about what?

HUSBAND:

About my sex life. My sex life has slowed
down considerably.

(This is not what the wife
said.)

THERAPIST:

Is that what she said?

HUSBAND:

That's what I said.

THERAPIST:

But is that what *she* said? Is that what she
just got done saying?

HUSBAND:

Yea, that's what she said.

THERAPIST:

Is that what you said?   (Therapist models how to
                                                check out communica-
                                                tion.)

WIFE:

What I'm saying is that he's feeling that
way. I know he hasn't slowed . . . he has
slowed down . . . and his age is some of it
. . . but most of it is those darn pills.

THERAPIST:

Well, what were you telling me? Were   (Therapist clarifies cod-
you telling me that the problem is sex, or   ing and decoding opera-
that you want affection when he's hearing   tions.)
you say sex?

WIFE:

I have told him that what I want a lot of
times is just for him to put his arms
around me and tell me he loves me.

THERAPIST:

When's the last time?

WIFE:

Last night. I always put my arms around
him and I tell him and I kiss him good
night and I tell him I love him every
night.

THERAPIST:

So how did that feel last night?

WIFE:

Well, it feels good to me. I don't know
how it feels to him.

THERAPIST:

Well, ask him.

WIFE:

I've asked him.

THERAPIST:

Well, ask him again. Let's see if he'll tell
you.

WIFE:

I'm asking you.

HUSBAND:

> [*Laughter*] I don't know. It's uppermost in
> my own thoughts anyhow.

THERAPIST:

> It's what?

HUSBAND:

> Uppermost in my own thoughts.

(A very unclear process of coding and decoding. The therapist feels confused.)

THERAPIST:

> What?

HUSBAND:

> The way she feels and acts.

THERAPIST:

> Could you be a little more clear about
> that? I'm confused about what you're say-
> ing.

(Therapist expresses his confusion directly.)

HUSBAND:

> My sex life has slowed down some and it
> has bothered me some, so naturally when
> she comes on anywhere along the line,
> well, that's what I think about.

THERAPIST:

> So you get to feeling crummy. So a lot of
> times when she asks for affection, you
> immediately start beating yourself over
> the head. Right?

At this point, the couple is exhibiting a repetitive transactional process that may explain why Mr. Smith has stopped taking his medication in the past. Mr. and Mrs. Smith both use sexual expression as the primary way to communicate intimacy and caring. When Mrs. Smith asks for caring, she asks in a way that Mr. Smith can easily distort and view as a request for sex. Mr. Smith also considers expression of intimacy as primarily a sexual matter and feels a resulting need to perform. The wife's expectation for affection is confused as a request for sex and since one side effect of Mr. Smith's medication is some decrease in sexual interest, Mr. Smith may decide to stop taking his medication. In the past, this may have resulted in a return of psychotic symptoms and another hospitalization. At this point, the therapist decides to concentrate on this issue by helping the couple learn to communicate clearly when either or both feel a desire for affection. The therapist also decides to continue in the middleman role as the couple is resisting talking directly to each other.

HUSBAND:
[*Laughs*] Partially, yes.

THERAPIST:
Okay, well how do you think you could work it out so the two of you could be at least affectionate without feeling crummy?

(Therapist makes a mistake. It would be better to suggest than to ask.)

HUSBAND:
Well, we understand about it but it is something I can't change.

THERAPIST:
I disagree with that, John.

HUSBAND:
I can quit that medicine tonight and get rid of all that trouble.

(A previously used solution?)

THERAPIST:
What I disagree with is that you say you can't stop interpreting every request of affection she makes as her wanting sex. You can change that.

HUSBAND:
Well, I do just about every time.

THERAPIST:
Okay, is that just because you believe she wants sex, or is that just your own confusion?

HUSBAND:
I believe she wants sex.

THERAPIST:
Okay, then that's something that you could check out . . . that you guys could get straight, see. You wouldn't have to feel crummy all of the time. That's a hell of a note to want to get close to your wife but then you feel crummy every time you get close to her.

(Therapist supports the husband through emotional accommodation and suggests an alternative.)

HUSBAND:

Yes . . .

THERAPIST:

Well, would you be willing to try to figure out some way that you wouldn't have to feel bad in that situation?

HUSBAND:

Yea, just tell me what to do.

THERAPIST:

Okay, how could she say it that you would believe her when she just wants affection?

HUSBAND:

I don't know . . . I don't know how I'd believe that.

THERAPIST:

Is there any way to believe that?

HUSBAND:

I suppose so. If I was doing a better job myself.

(Husband discounts himself.)

THERAPIST:

Do you think that she'd lie to you?

HUSBAND:

No.

THERAPIST:

Okay, so if you wanted affection from John right now, how would you go about telling him?

(Therapist attempts to bring the issue into the present.)

WIFE:

Well, I've told him.

THERAPIST:

· I mean right now, if you wanted affection right now, how would you tell him? Let's see how you'd go about telling him right now. I want to follow this because there seems to be some confusion here.

WIFE:

All right. When we are lying in bed at night, well, when he gets in bed he always turns his back to me, mainly because he can't sleep on his right shoulder. I would reach over and put my arm on him and I

want him to turn over and put his arms
around me and just hold me.

THERAPIST:
Do you ever do that in the day?

WIFE:
I've told him that too.

THERAPIST:
Do you ever do that in the day?

WIFE:
Yes.

THERAPIST:
What, just hold each other?

WIFE:
Yea.

THERAPIST:
Well, how does that go when you hold
each other during the day?

WIFE:
I just walk up to him and make him stand
there and I put my arms around him and
hold him.

THERAPIST:
Okay, well how does he know you're not
coming on sexual?

WIFE:
Because I don't feel all over him like I   (Wife tells therapist how
would if I was in bed at night.   she adds confusion to the
                                                  process.)
THERAPIST:
Well, let's check that out. When she does
that during the day, what do you feel she
is wanting from you?

HUSBAND:
Oh, nothing. Just a little affection.

THERAPIST:
Do you feel crummy then?

HUSBAND:
No.

THERAPIST:
For real?

HUSBAND:
Yes, for real.

THERAPIST:
Okay, so there is a way she can get a little   (Therapist shows that

affection from you without your feeling crummy.

HUSBAND:

Yes, in the middle of the day.

THERAPIST:

Well, what happens in the middle of the day that is different from the night?

HUSBAND:

I guess we aren't alone. I don't know.

WIFE:

The kids are in school.

HUSBAND:

Somebody's always hanging around.

WIFE:

We can always expect someone to come to the door. Yes.

THERAPIST:

I think this is really important.

WIFE:

So do I. It's been bothering me.

THERAPIST:

There are two things I'm concerned about. Number one, I'm worried about John putting himself down. Because a hell of a lot of that is the medicine. It's like a bad situation because to control some of the anxiety you have some medicine, but that also has its side effects. But you are putting yourself down because the medicine is doing something to you. Do you see what I'm saying?

HUSBAND:

Yea.

THERAPIST:

You are beating yourself over the head for a medicine side effect.

WIFE:

For a long time I thought it was me and he just didn't want me until I realized that it wasn't.

THERAPIST:

So that is one problem—that you are put-

(there is an interactional alternative.)

(Husband and wife both discount the alternative.)

(The therapist is somewhat nervous as he doesn't want to lose this opportunity. The therapist makes a little speech to handle his anxiety.)

(Therapist supports husband.)

ting yourself down for something that is not your fault. Right?

HUSBAND:

Yea, I guess so.

THERAPIST:

Then the other problem is that how can the two of you have some affection for each other without you thinking she just wants sex?

HUSBAND:

I don't know what to say about that.

THERAPIST:

Is there any way she could give you a message that would be real clear to you? Sometimes she hints around.

HUSBAND:

Yea, no, I don't know any way to make it clear.

(Husband and wife are in agreement and are joined against the therapist.)

He knows how I feel, and he knows when I start that that is when I really want him to make love to me. But, when I just put my arm around him and kiss him good night, he should know the difference in that.

(What "should be" is not the point. This is a way of continuing the confusion.)

THERAPIST:

Apparently he doesn't. See what I'm getting is the way you communicate by not talking. See you have all these little signals that you think each other understand. But that is getting all confused. All these little signals are getting all confused. He is not sure what they mean. Like, when he turns over and backs away from you, you confuse that and say, well, that means he doesn't care about me anymore. What he is really saying is, "I really feel crummy and rotten about this."

WIFE:

Yea, I see what you mean.

THERAPIST:

So you got all these little signals that

aren't working anymore. So how could you change that?

HUSBAND:

Quit the medicine.

THERAPIST:

No, how could you quit the confusion about that? All those little underlying messages that you aren't sure what they mean anymore?

(Therapist clarifies his message.)

HUSBAND:

Well, I suppose I'm too uptight.

THERAPIST:

What I suggest is that you say it out loud. Say what it is you want out loud.

WIFE:

He does tell me and I don't tell him. He comes plain out and tells me no.

THERAPIST:

Are you hearing what I'm saying?

WIFE:

I'm trying.

THERAPIST:

What did I say?

WIFE:

You said something about . . .

THERAPIST:

Rather than hint around about what you want, why don't you come out and say it? See, you hint around about wanting affection, and he gets that mixed up with your wanting sex.

WIFE:

Yea, well sometimes I do tell him, "Turn over and put your arm around me."

THERAPIST:

Turn over and put your arm around me because right now, I want sex, or, because right now I want affection?

(Therapist suggests an alternative.)

WIFE:

That's not always why I want him to put his arm around me.

(This seems like resistance to the therapist.)

THERAPIST:

Which is it?

WIFE:

It's neither one of them sometimes.
Sometimes it's that I'm afraid.

THERAPIST:

So another way you could do it would be,   (Therapist suggests an al-
"John, turn around and put your arms   ternative.)
around me because I want (a) sex, (b) af-
fection, or (c) I'm scared."

WIFE:

I didn't want him to think I was scared.

THERAPIST:

Well.   (Therapist feels frus-
                                                trated.)

WIFE:

Cause there is times when I am. Since his
father passed away there has been times I
have been real afraid.

THERAPIST:

I think that would be something that you
could change that would be helpful to
you. Saying it out loud.

WIFE:

I didn't want him to think I was afraid of   (Yet the wife is saying it.
his father.   Another double mes-
                                                sage.)

THERAPIST:

Would you be willing to say that out loud
so he wouldn't have to guess?

WIFE:

Yea, I'll try and say it.

THERAPIST:

Okay, would that be helpful to you?

HUSBAND:

Yea, I suppose so.   (The husband may not
                                                be sure he wants to feel
                                                better about this issue.
                                                Things have been con-
                                                fused for quite a period of
                                                time and such a change
                                                may feel very frighten-
                                                ing.)

THERAPIST:

What do you think?

HUSBAND:

Yea, I guess.

THERAPIST:

Do you want to role play that or try to practice it for a minute?

HUSBAND:

I'll try.

THERAPIST:

Okay, what do you want from her right now?

HUSBAND:

Nothing.

THERAPIST:

Why not?

HUSBAND:

There isn't anything I want right now in any way, shape, or form.

(Husband does appear to be angry. The therapist is very sure at this point that resistance is emerging.)

THERAPIST:

Okay, what do you want from him right now?

WIFE:

I didn't want to hear him say that.

THERAPIST:

All right, tell him.

WIFE:

I never want to hear him say that, that he never wants anything from me. I'd like to have him walk up and ask me to tell him I love him, like I do him. I know he loves me but I want to hear him say it.

THERAPIST:

Okay, so . . .

(Therapist attempts to get the couple to do in the interview what they have stated they will do at home.)

WIFE:

But he never tells me that.

THERAPIST:

So what do you want from him right now?

WIFE:

Right now?

THERAPIST:

Would you like to hear that right now?

WIFE:

Well, sure. I'd love to hear it right now.

THERAPIST:

Why don't you ask him about it?

WIFE:

Would you tell me you love me?   (Wife sends a clear message.)

HUSBAND:

I love you. I really do love you.   (Husband's message is congruent and clear.)

WIFE:

I ask him that once in a while in bed.

THERAPIST:

How did that sound?

WIFE:

To me, he said it because we are sitting   (Wife discounts husband's message.)
here and I had to ask him.

THERAPIST:

Well, you do have to ask him if he's not
doing it and you want it.

WIFE:

I didn't want to have to ask him that way.

THERAPIST:

Why not?

WIFE:

There is a different way of asking a per-   (The wife believes that he should be able to read her mind.)
son.

THERAPIST:

You'd rather hint around then.

WIFE:

No, but to hint around about it—I've got
a good way of doing that. [*Laughter*]

THERAPIST:

But that has caused you guys some problems.

WIFE:

I know that.

THERAPIST:

> Okay, let's try it again. Let's see if we can work it out. I think she is really wanting to hear that, John. Is that important to you?

WIFE:

> Sure. I want him to put some feeling behind it. There wasn't any feeling behind that, when he said it that time.

THERAPIST:

> I thought there was a lot of feeling behind it.

(The therapist felt that the husband had said it with feeling.)

WIFE:

> [*With laughter*] You really wouldn't want me to tell you what I'm thinking right now either.

(Wife changes subject.)

THERAPIST:

> Sure I do.

(The therapist falls for the wife's ploy and the subject gets changed.)

WIFE:

> All the way over here I was trying to figure why you always want me to come over here. Because to me, you are not doing me any good.

THERAPIST:

> No?

WIFE:

> No. That's what I told my husband. That's what I said. I didn't think I wanted to come over here with him any more because you are not doing me any good.

(A process has been challenged and at this point, resistance occurs.)

THERAPIST:

> What do you want me to do?

WIFE:

> I don't know. I want my husband helped. He isn't getting any better in my book. Still in the mornings he's walking around facing that. And he still does this quite a bit, maybe not here, but at home and that still bothers me.

(Wife attempts to put husband in the patient position.)

THERAPIST:

> So what do you want me to do?

WIFE:

I don't know what I want you to do. I
want some doctors to help him.

THERAPIST:

What do you want the doctors to do?

WIFE:

I don't know. They can't make a miracle,
I know that. And I know John has to try,
too.

THERAPIST:

Let me tell you a couple of things I'd like
you to do.

(Therapist changes the
subject.)

WIFE:

If I can help him, I'd sure do it.

THERAPIST:

The first thing I'd like you to do is to quit
hinting around to John as to what it is you
want because he seems to be getting confused as to whether you want sex or
whether you want affection or what it is
you want. That's one thing I'd like to see
you do.

WIFE:

I'll do it. If I think it's going to help him.
I'll be willing to do it.

(Yes, no,—I'll do that.
Another double mes-
sage.)

THERAPIST:

The other thing I'd like you to do is that I
would like for you to quit taking care of
him as much as you do.

WIFE:

Mister, that's gonna be hard to do because
I love him so much . . . I'd do anything
under the sun for him if he wanted me to.

THERAPIST:

Except that one thing that would be most
helpful to him, which is not to take care
of him as much as you do.

(Therapist   confronts
wife.)

WIFE:

I know it's hurting him for me to do too
much for him.

THERAPIST:

That's right. We've mentioned that before.

WIFE:

> I know.

THERAPIST:

> Well?

WIFE:

> How do you do it after you've done it for sixteen years?

THERAPIST:

> It's hard as hell.   (Therapist supports wife.)

WIFE:

> It is. It's easy to say and it's hard to do.

THERAPIST:

> Okay.

WIFE:

> Well, I can try. I don't know if I can do it or not, but all I can say is I can try.

THERAPIST:

> So, see it's going to be doubly important because about the time he starts getting up and leaving in the morning to go to this training program, it's going to be a different thing for you.

WIFE:

> I know.

THERAPIST:

> I've got one other question to ask you. How long have you been feeling that way?

WIFE:

> How long have I been feeling this way about you?

THERAPIST:

> Yes.

WIFE:

> Well . . .

THERAPIST:

> How long?

WIFE:

> It's been about five or six months.

THERAPIST:

> I've got a question.   (Therapist wants the couple to send accurate messages to him.)

WIFE:

> All right. Do I like you or not?

THERAPIST:

I'm quite positive right now you got mad at me.

WIFE:

No, I'm not mad at you. I think you're a pretty nice guy.

THERAPIST:

You're frustrated with me.

WIFE:

Yes.

THERAPIST:

Okay, why didn't you tell me that? It took you five months.

WIFE:

I don't know. I've been upset. Especially about John and my sex life and the other. Getting him to show he cares.

THERAPIST:

When was the last time you had sex?

WIFE:

The other night.

HUSBAND:

Two nights ago. Didn't stop just slowed down.

THERAPIST:

Okay, would you be willing to start trying to communicate with each other differently?

(Therapist attempts to get a contract so he can try to operationalize the contract within the interview.)

WIFE:

Yes, if I think it will do any good.

THERAPIST:

Well, do you?

WIFE:

I don't know if it will or not. I'd have to try to find out, wouldn't I?

THERAPIST:

Well?

WIFE:

Okay.

THERAPIST:

Okay, the deal I want to make then is for

(Therapist clearly states

you two to talk clearly to each other instead of all this hinting around business.

WIFE:

Mainly, why I hint around a lot is because I don't want him mad at me.

THERAPIST:

Well, you've got to get over that.

HUSBAND:

Take somebody as dumb as me, well, the hinting around is worse than telling it right out.

THERAPIST:

Are you saying that you're too dumb to understand hints?

(Checks out husband's coding. Again, the therapist models the process.)

HUSBAND:

Uh huh.

THERAPIST:

So am I, John.

(Therapist offers support.)

[*Silence*]

THERAPIST:

It's really hard for me to understand when people are hinting around. It's hard for me to understand when you hint around. That's just natural.

WIFE:

Do they have family counseling here?

(Wife changes the subject to include kids.)

THERAPIST:

Yes.

WIFE:

Well, let me tell you something. There is so much fighting and friction at our house that he ain't gonna get any better. I've got two daughters and most of the time when they fight is at dishes time. And if John don't sit at that table with a belt, or if I'm not over there beating them with a belt, they'll fight. They can't look at each other without it. There is only one kid in our

(what he wants the couple to do.)

home that everyone gets along with, and I mean everybody, and that is my youngest son.

THERAPIST:

So you would like to get the kids in here, too?

WIFE:

I'd like for them to come plain and tell, they're not afraid to tell us, in fact I can't get them to shut up. They think they have to have the last word. That just drives me up the wall because John used to help me with my first three, which aren't his. They're his. I didn't mean to say it that way. They are his. I mean, we made them mind a heck of alot better than we do the last two we've got right now, cause they get away with everything and anything. All they have to do is shed one tear and they've got it.

THERAPIST:

Do you hint around with them?

WIFE:

Do I hint around with them? There is no hinting to it.

(Therapist wants to concentrate on the marital couple and tries to show that not hinting around with each other will also be valuable when talking to the kids. At a later point the therapist plans on bringing in the children.)

THERAPIST:

I think you are wrong.

WIFE:

You think I ought to hint around with them?

THERAPIST:

No, I think you do too much.

WIFE:

I give in to them too much.

THERAPIST:

> That is what I mean. That's hinting around.

WIFE:

> And when the other kids come in they like to pick at the younger ones. And I tell them to leave them alone because if they tell their father, their father gets mad at the older two, and they got such hot tempers that they go to mouthing off and may just take off. I want my family to be together.

THERAPIST:

> Okay.

WIFE:

> I've never seen a family the way mine is.

THERAPIST:

> All right, you are willing to try to improve how the two of you talk to each other because there are so many misunderstandings. What is happening between the two of you is you're thinking he is feeling one way and he's thinking you are feeling another way that is different from how you really feel.

(Therapist again clarifies what he thinks is going on.)

WIFE:

> We are fighting a losing battle. That's what we are doing.

THERAPIST:

> You are losing track of where you are.

(Therapist relabels.)

WIFE:

> Yea, but it's better today, but I don't know why we can't do it at home. Why we have to come to some office to do it.

THERAPIST:

> You did do better today.

(Therapist offers support.)

WIFE:

> I act like I have to have someone to be a defense or an in-between person to help stop whatever is going on.

(Wife explains that she does understand that the difficulty her husband is having is in part a result

of the communication
problems between the
two of them.)

In this interview, the therapist concentrated upon helping the couple send clearer messages and make more accurate evaluations of the messages they received. Most of the interventions were made from the middleman role. The couple has continued in conjoint therapy and Mr. Smith has remained out of the hospital for over three years. His medication has been significantly reduced. At the time of this writing, he is also working full time and the children are doing well in school.

5

Mr. and Mrs. Jones: Getting Closer Together

The Jones couple requested marital counseling complaining of frequent arguments, a less than satisfactory sexual relationship, and a recognition that both marital members were wanting to spend more and more time away from each other. Mr. Jones was in law school, Mrs. Jones was a teacher, and both stated that they had been having problems for about two years. The couple exhibited an interactional style that included an overly intellectualizing husband and a wife who either withdrew or acted out to get her husband's attention. Both marital members used a number of interactional ploys to avoid intimacy. The following vignette is an excerpt from the sixth conjoint therapy session, and represents a turning point in the couple's relationship. The therapist's focus is centered around interrupting every attempt made by the couple to avoid contact and intimacy within the conjoint session.

WIFE:

Why did we change so much?

(Wife often uses an over-interest in "Why?" to

avoid intimacy in the present. The therapist interrupts this transactional sequence before it begins.)

THERAPIST:

I Don't know. Why did you change so much?

WIFE:

I don't know. I guess different experiences make me unhappy with my marriage.

THERAPIST:

Okay. What do you want to do about it?

WIFE:

I don't know. I guess stop blaming him for all of the things that happen.

THERAPIST:

Well, do you want to communicate with him or not?

(The therapist is rather confrontive right from the beginning as he is confident that a good relationship exists between himself and the couple.)

WIFE:

[*Laughs*] Sometimes no.

THERAPIST:

How about right now?

WIFE:

I'll make a stab at it.

THERAPIST:

You'll make a stab at it. What do you want to say to him?

WIFE:

First I'll put my feet on the floor and stop laughing. I'm nervous now.

(Wife has developed some insight into how she often used body posture to block communication.)

HUSBAND:

Is that bad?

WIFE:

Yes. That means we are not communicating.

THERAPIST:

No, it is not bad. I just want you to be aware of how you keep yourself from feeling things and how you keep yourself from talking to people. It's not bad. It's just a thing you do that doesn't work very well.

HUSBAND:

Everyone does that.

THERAPIST:

Sometimes it keeps you from talking to him.

(Therapist supports the wife.)

[*Wife laughs.*]

HUSBAND:

You see, I move around so much I can't sit still. It is a nervous habit.

WIFE:

I'll communicate with him. You feel unhappy, don't you? You look sad. [*Looks at therapist.*]

(The wife is not saying anything about herself as a person.)

THERAPIST:

I don't. You ask him. I don't feel sad.

(Wife was looking at therapist as she was talking to her husband.)

WIFE:

Are you sad?

HUSBAND:

I don't think I'm sad.

WIFE:

You look unhappy.

HUSBAND:

I think you are feeling better today than you have all week, aren't you?

(Husband changes subject to wife in an attempt to keep from stating something about himself. Both the husband and the wife attempt to get the other to say how they feel.)

THERAPIST:

Well, how did we get to her when she is asking you about how you feel?

HUSBAND:
> That's a good question. I don't feel sad.
> No.

THERAPIST:
> Tell Betty how you feel.

HUSBAND:
> I feel like . . . I feel . . . I feel like you
> . . . that isn't how I feel, is it? I feel happy
> that you seem to feel good. Is that how I
> feel?

(Husband gets confused when he attempts to say something about self. He usually focuses upon how his wife feels. This helps keep wife in the sick role.)

THERAPIST:
> I don't know.

HUSBAND:
> Well, I mean is that telling? If I said that
> to someone is that the impression they
> would get about how I feel?

THERAPIST:
> Well, I don't know. Why don't you check
> it out with her and see if she got the mes-
> sage.

HUSBAND:
> Did you get the message?

(Husband checks it out.)

WIFE:
> How you felt? No.

HUSBAND:
> You didn't?

WIFE:
> Well, how you felt about me. Yea, I guess
> so. Jeff gets all upset lately because what
> we are trying to do is play this game that
> we tell each other what we should and
> shouldn't do.

(Wife changes her mind and reinforces her husband for an unclear message.)

HUSBAND:
> Like this morning, everytime I'd say
> something, she gets mad and tells me
> what I should have said. And then she
> says something and I tell her what she
> should have said and we are so concerned
> with what the other person should have

(Husband describes the couple's game.)

said to us that we aren't listening to what
we are saying. And it is a big game.

THERAPIST:

What does that game do for you.

HUSBAND:

Nothing, except pull us apart and make
us angry at each other.

THERAPIST:

Okay, so it pulls you apart and what it
does for you is it keeps you from getting
together. Right?

(A game designed to
avoid intimacy.)

HUSBAND:

Right.

THERAPIST:

Well, how are you going to do that in
here? Are you going to talk to me? Is that
going to get you together or are you going
to talk to each other?

(Therapist points out that
the game is occuring
within the interview.)

HUSBAND:

Well, we can talk to you, too. I don't
think we can always talk to each other.

THERAPIST:

Talk to her about it. I mean, you've got
this problem, you guys play these games
. . .

WIFE:

How do we start?

HUSBAND:

Just when I say something to you that you
don't like, tell me, but you don't have to
get angry.

(Husband tells wife what
she can do. He does not
tell what he can do. This
helps reinforce wife's sick
role.)

THERAPIST:

That is what she could do. What could
you do?

HUSBAND:

She didn't ask me what I could do. But I
started with what she could do.

WIFE:

So you immediately told me what I could
do.

(Wife is beginning to
catch on.)

[Laughter]

HUSBAND:

[Laughing] I'll tell you what you can do, goddamnit? What could we do? Not get pissed off at each other for saying things that are so innocuous and not worth getting angry about.

(Husband sees what happened and makes a joke.)

THERAPIST:

That is what you can stop doing, okay? What can you start doing?

(The couple also focuses on what is wrong rather than what they could do.)

HUSBAND:

We can start talking to each other and talking to each other about what we are saying and not talk to each other about what we are not saying.

(Both husband and wife usually focus on what to stop doing rather than what they could start doing.)

THERAPIST:

What could you do right now?

[Silence]

THERAPIST:

Notice your posture. Notice how you are talking to her. Does that mean you really want to be close to her?

(Therapist comments on husband's nonverbal messages. The husband's posture is leaning back and away from his wife.)

HUSBAND:

It probably shows that I am unconcerned with what I am doing. I don't know what it shows.

THERAPIST:

How do you feel when he's talking to you sitting like that? Do you think he wants to be close?

WIFE:

I am so used to his sitting that way and slouching that usually I just yell at him and tell him he should sit up straight or something.

(The wife yells at her husband rather than telling him how she decodes his nonverbal messages. She does not check it out.)

WIFE:

I get mad at him just . . . But I just never thought of it as being away from me. You know what I mean? I never looked at it that way. I don't feel when the two of us are together we are communicating with each other at all or being close. I never get that feeling and when he talks to me lately, I get all upset and I shouldn't, and I don't know why it bothers me the way he talks to me. I'm just trying to say how I feel. I don't know why I do. That he is talking to me or at me and that we aren't talking to each other, you know, like a caring husband and wife.

(The wife expresses how she has been feeling lately.)

THERAPIST:

So what do you want from him right now?

WIFE:

I don't know.

THERAPIST:

Do you want him to be closer or far away?

WIFE:

I am afraid.

THERAPIST:

What are you afraid of?

(This is a clear and congruent message.)

WIFE:

I'm afraid of getting close.

THERAPIST:

Well, tell him that.

WIFE:

But I used to not be afraid of getting close.

(Wife gets nervous and returns to her focus on "why"?)

THERAPIST:

Okay, well, that is "used to," right? Now how are you feeling? Right now?

HUSBAND:

She told me that in the car on the way down here. You told me that you were afraid of getting close.

(Husband answers for his wife.)

WIFE:

Well, I've been very afraid lately. Afraid

of getting close to you . . . just even . . . I mean physically and emotionally. I'm tending to just remain apart from you.

HUSBAND:

So many of the small things that you do upset me, and so many of the small things that I do upset you. Sometimes it is difficult thinking of those things. We get upset about those things as though it is the whole feeling. The whole feeling that when I eat fast or make some noise eating you don't like that, or some of the other things I do. Like I don't take out the garbage and some other things so it is hard for you to get close to me because you remember the little things that I do that seem to show I don't care. And it is the same with me with some of the things that you do that make me feel that you don't care, and it makes it hard for me, I guess, to feel that you care.

(Husband begins to express some of his concerns in a less intellectualizing way.)

THERAPIST:

So you are concerned about her not caring.

(Therapist helps husband word it more clearly.)

HUSBAND:

To a certain extent.

THERAPIST:

Talk to her about that.

HUSBAND:

I started to.

THERAPIST:

Tell her about how you are worried about her not caring and how scared you are.

HUSBAND:

Well, we have gone over this before.

(Husband starts to back out of expressing his concerns.)

THERAPIST:

Yea, I know you have gone over it before, but the way you go about going over it is what concerns me. We don't need a running detail of all the little things if you

(Therapist tells husband how to say it in a clearer way.)

stick to your feelings, like "I am kind of scared," or "I sometimes think that you don't care about me." If you could just tell her those things instead of getting into all those details.

HUSBAND:

I sometimes say those things and she is less receptive than she is in here. The other night, she said, "You don't want to be close to me, you are pushing me away." I said, "I want to be close to you. I may be pushing you away, but I want to be close to you." And she said, "No you don't."

(Husband wants to talk about the past to avoid the fact that his wife is receptive right now.)

THERAPIST:

Well, which do you want right now?

(Therapist redirects the focus to the present.)

HUSBAND:

I want to be close to her. I just sometimes don't come across that way.

THERAPIST:

So could you do that right now?

HUSBAND:

How could I get close or how could I tell her? By showing some concern about what she is talking about?

[*Silence*]

HUSBAND:

She is busy with her cooking and I am busy with my job.

(Husband gets anxious and intellectualizes.)

THERAPIST:

There ain't no stoves right now.

(Therapist redirects to the present.)

[*Silence*]

THERAPIST:

You don't know how to get close to her, do you?

HUSBAND:

How to get close?

THERAPIST:

Yea. We are talking about closeness, and you immediately go into all these nervous things.

(Therapist demonstrates by simulating husband's body posture.)

HUSBAND:

I'm like that even if we don't talk about closeness.

THERAPIST:

No.

HUSBAND:

I'm not?

(The husband only does this within the interview when he is close to expressing feelings.)

THERAPIST:

No.

WIFE:

Yes, he is.

(Wife rescues the husband.)

HUSBAND:

You mean I sit straight and listen to you and I never sit like this?

THERAPIST:

No. What I am getting at is that this is one of the ways that you keep yourself from getting close to her.

(Therapist restates his point.)

HUSBAND:

Well, I probably keep myself from being close to everybody. Cause I am always like that. Because I am nervous and I'm active and I have to be doing something so I can't keep my body still. I didn't know that was a sign of not being close to people.

THERAPIST:

That's what I think.

HUSBAND:

So if you are close to someone, that means you don't act unconcerned, is that what you are saying?

THERAPIST:

I'm just saying that is not working out very

(Therapist realizes that

well for you. We have been at this for quite awhile and you don't get close to her. You just talk about details rather than getting close to her and talking about how you feel. You don't let her know you.

HUSBAND:

What does that have to do with it?

THERAPIST:

It is awfully hard to talk to anyone in any intimate way when you are way the hell back like that. Your body posture tells you a lot.

[Therapist demonstrates husband's posture.]

HUSBAND:

You mean if I sat like this it would mean . . .

THERAPIST:

I think it would help you out. .

HUSBAND:

Why, because I am closer physically?

HUSBAND:

Well, because I was telling you that we're close like this sometimes at home on the couch. Then we start talking to each other and something happens. Either I bitch about something she is doing, or I'm talking with her and I ignore her to a certain extent when the dog is there and I play with him and I look at him and I don't look at her.

THERAPIST:

Do you rub the dog's head?

HUSBAND:

Yea.

THERAPIST:

Oh, do you? Does the dog like it? Well, that's good. You have gotten the idea.

HUSBAND:

But sometimes the dog is jumping up and I'll pet him and I'll be talking to Betty and looking at Betty and I'm only petting him

(he has been arguing with the husband. This is an example of countertransference.)

(Therapist continues to act out his frustration.)

(What happens is just what did happen.)

(Husband brings in the family dog to avoid intimacy.)

(Husband has right idea, but the wrong object for affection.)

to keep him from jumping and licking me
in the face.

THERAPIST:

This week I want you to talk to the dog
and pet Betty.

(Therapist presents an alternative in the hopes
that the husband will get
the point. Provocative
exaggeration.)

HUSBAND:

The dog doesn't talk to me. The dog
doesn't communicate with me.

THERAPIST:

Get a babysitter for the dog.

WIFE:

I think sometimes he feels safer with the
dog than he does with me. Because the
dog doesn't yell at him and get angry with
him.

THERAPIST:

Why don't you ask him how safe he feels
now?

(Therapist redirects conversation back to the present.)

WIFE:

How safe do you feel now that the dog is
not here?

HUSBAND:

The dog doesn't have to be here.

WIFE:

It is just that we really don't sit down and
talk to each other that often and go over
things. And then when we do I feel like
the dog comes near cause he wants your
attention and he doesn't want to be ignored.

(Couple goes back to talking about the dog. Again,
the function is to avoid
intimacy.)

[Therapist snores, acts bored and
unconcerned.]

(Therapist attempts to
demonstrate the point in
a more experiential
manner.)

HUSBAND:

Well, now, all right. That is different.
You are not talking back to me.

THERAPIST:

Yea, I'm ignoring the hell out of you.

Like if you were talking to me and I'm sitting like this and I'm bored and I'm looking away, what are you going to think? Are you going to think I'm interested in you?

HUSBAND:

No.

THERAPIST:

Okay. Sort of like your mouth says one thing, "I want to be close," but all your mannerisms are real far away.

WIFE:

I think in a way I feel like I have sometimes pushed him to be that way. I mean I'm not . . . I tell him so many times that I hate him and I don't love him anymore that I have almost backed him into a wall like that.

(The wife jumps in to rescue the husband.)

THERAPIST:

So you have helped him stay that way.

(Therapist reframes wife's statement in a way that doesn't let the husband off the hook.)

WIFE:

Yes.

THERAPIST:

Now, do you want to do that right now?

WIFE:

No.

THERAPIST:

Okay, so what do you want to help him do?

WIFE:

Well, part of me wants to and a part of me doesn't want to. Like part of me wants to keep my job and a part of me doesn't want to.

(Wife gets anxious.)

THERAPIST:

Let's forget about that part that doesn't want to be close to him for a second, and concentrate on the part that does.

(Therapist counters the wife's attempt to remain distant.)

[Husband moves his chair closer to his wife.]

WIFE:

> [*Giggling*] It does feel nicer when you sit that way.

THERAPIST:

> Move your chair over a little bit closer, and maybe he'll feel a little bit nicer too.

(Therapist helps wife reward husband for his change.)

[*Wife laughs.*]

HUSBAND:

> We get close like this . . .

THERAPIST:

> You just did it again.

HUSBAND:

> Jim, I don't . . .

THERAPIST:

> You get her right close by and start talking to me.

(Husband talks to the therapist after the wife moves closer)

HUSBAND:

> He doesn't.

WIFE:

> I know, but then I see you giving him the attention I want.

HUSBAND:

> I don't give him an overly amount of attention. Do I come home and go right to him and ignore you? In fact, I come in the house now and I ignore him completely and he goes away from me when I come out to the kitchen to talk to you, and I never even pet him and he goes back to sleep.

(This process represents the couple's way of avoiding each other.)

WIFE:

> That is why I say when he comes up, if you just ignore him when he is there, he is not going to jump all over us.

HUSBAND:

> When we are sitting here on the couch I pet him to keep him from jumping onto the couch.

[*Therapist laughs.*]

HUSBAND:

> What is the matter? You are sitting over there laughing.

THERAPIST:

Christ, you've got the dog running over the couch and the two of you are sitting there talking about this . . . Oh Lord . . . it is the meaningless details that you all use to keep yourselves away from each other.

(Therapist confronts the couple with their avoidance.)

HUSBAND:

What—talking about this stuff?

THERAPIST:

Yea.

HUSBAND:

Why?

THERAPIST:

Why don't you show her how you care for her?

HUSBAND:

Why do people talk about that all the time? Can't they talk about some of the things that go on in the house that make the atmosphere . . .

THERAPIST:

You seldom show caring. You talk about so many details.

(Therapist points out the issue.)

HUSBAND:

Right now we are having a conversation about being close and some of the things that keep us from being close.

(Husband is angry.)

THERAPIST:

You can talk about that forever and you'll still not be close.

HUSBAND:

Perhaps that is right. But even the fact that we are sitting here talking about the situation when I come home from school, sitting on the couch, and talking with one another about what goes on, then we are communicating; then we are close.

THERAPIST:

Why don't you check that out with her and see if she feels close and she'd like to do that, or if she would like to talk about something else?

HUSBAND:

Do you like to talk about that or is there something else that you would like to talk about that would make you feel closer? . . Can't people talk about things that are on their minds? You are saying that we are going to continue to talk about it and nothing else but details. Well, what do people do? Do they go home and say how do you feel about me today?

(Husband does not check it out. He doesn't wait for her to answer.)

THERAPIST:

Sure they do.

HUSBAND:

Do you love me today like you did yesterday? Will you sit on the couch with me and whisper sweet nothings is my ear?

WIFE:

Yes! That would be nice!

(Wife likes this idea.)

HUSBAND:

People talk about details.

THERAPIST:

What did she just say?

(Therapist reinforces the wife.)

HUSBAND:

That would be nice? Okay, when I come home from school I will sit on the couch and whisper sweet nothings in your ear. [Laughter]

("When I get home" is another way to avoid intimacy.)

THERAPIST:

Why not now?

HUSBAND:

Not in the mood now.

THERAPIST:

Why aren't you in the mood now?

HUSBAND:

I have a headache.

THERAPIST:

Bull shit. You are so damn slippery. I hate having attorneys for clients.

(Therapist confronts the husband.)

HUSBAND:

You hate having attorneys for clients! I'm not an attorney yet.

THERAPIST:

Well, you almost are and you are going to be a good one.

HUSBAND:

Slippery as hell, but honest.

THERAPIST:

Well, you are not very honest about your feelings.

HUSBAND:

[Confused and stutters] That has nothing to do with being honest in my sense of what I was just talking about. Being dishonest with my feelings is not because I'm trying to mislead anyone or mislead myself. It is because I'm incapable of putting my feelings into words, and I always have been. I've never been an emotional person.

(Husband expresses *his* problem for the first time in the interview.)

THERAPIST:

But that won't work. Get your ass off the back of that chair and get your face to Betty.

HUSBAND:

My face *was* close to Betty and you started talking to me and I'm getting away from you.

(Husband is angry.)

THERAPIST:

Fine. I'll move back and you've got me out of the picture. You can just get close to Betty. [Moves chair away from the couple.]

HUSBAND:

Well, then why is there anything wrong with us talking about the things that are at home when I come home from school?

(Husband addresses the therapist after he just told the therapist to get away.)

THERAPIST:

There is nothing wrong with it, but you do it all the time. Do something in addition.

WIFE:

Because it is not talking about you and me.

HUSBAND:

Well, maybe it's . . . it's talking about me and you. Maybe that is. We don't talk about me and you enough and first of all.

WIFE:

Instead of talking about the negative things that cause trouble . . .

HUSBAND:

We are not talking about the negative things . . .

WIFE:

We should talk about the things that we could do to make things work.

HUSBAND:

And we were trying to talk about getting over the hurdle of being jealous of Jet when I should be concerning myself with you. I'm concerning myself with Jet.

(Jet is the couple's dog.)

WIFE:

No. That is talking about the negative things that we want to get over. Let's talk about the things we want to do. I always said I'd like to go bike riding with you and get out and do things.

(Wife reaches out to husband.)

HUSBAND:

We tried last week and what happened?

[*Wife laughs.*]

HUSBAND:

Don't look at him. Now we are going back to details. Don't give me any of that crap. If she tells me that she wants to do things, okay. We tried to do one of the things she wants to do.

(Husband shows that he is getting the idea.)

THERAPIST:

So far, you have brought the dog in this office, you have brought the goddamn bicycles in this office. You have got this perfectly attractive young lady over here who wants you to whisper sweet nothings in her ear and you are talking about bicycles and dogs.

(Therapist suggests an alternative.)

HUSBAND:

Who brought up the bicycles in this conversation?

[*Silence*]

HUSBAND:

She did. She said I want to do some of the
things I like to do, and she said she'd like
to go bicycle riding, and I said then let's
go bicycle riding one day.

(This is not what hap-
pened.)

WIFE:

What do I want to do? You are angry at
me and I . . .

HUSBAND:

No, I'm not angry at you. I'm angry with
him. I'm not angry at you at all.

THERAPIST:

He is getting mad at me, Betty. Don't let
that worry you. It is not you.

(Therapist supports the
wife.)

HUSBAND:

Because I think we are communicating
and we are not communicating the way
he wants us to . . .

THERAPIST:

You are right. You are not communicating the way I want you to.

HUSBAND:

And I am not so sure . . .

WIFE:

The reason he brought that up is because
. . .

HUSBAND:

We are not talking about that. Let's not
talk about that. I don't want to talk about
that. I don't think we should talk about
the reason I brought that up. We don't
need to justify in his mind what I was
talking about.

(Husband is very mad at
the therapist.)

WIFE:

I want to explain it because that is where
we get into trouble. When something
happens that turns out negative, you don't

want to try it again because you say, well,
we tried this and you get all pissed off so
let's not try it again. We can't do that. We
have to just try until maybe the next time,
it won't happen again.

THERAPIST:

What do you want him to do right now?

WIFE:

I want him to sit closer to me.   (Wife sends a clear mes-
                                                   sage.)

THERAPIST:

Sit closer to you?

WIFE:

Yes.

HUSBAND:

I agree with you that there are certain
ways that we should talk with each other
and certain ways we shouldn't, but I don't
think you can take someone who has
never been in the water and throw them
in the deep and say swim.

THERAPIST:

So you think I'm pushing you too hard.   (Therapist checks out his
                                                decoding.)

HUSBAND:

I think you are trying to get us to talk
about something we are not ready to talk
about right now.

THERAPIST:

But I don't want you to talk about any-   (Therapist supports the
thing. I want you to shut up and start   husband.)
whispering sweet nothings in her ear.

HUSBAND:

No, I don't want to . . .

THERAPIST:

Is he close enough for you?

[*Wife laughs.*]

HUSBAND:

Am I close enough for you?

THERAPIST:

I think you'd better grab his leg or he is

going to run away.

[*Husband moves chair closer to wife.*]

HUSBAND:

What is wrong? I'm asking you this, what is wrong with our just talking about whatever we want to talk about?

THERAPIST:

You sit back in the corner with your legs up . . .

HUSBAND:

We have gotten over that hurdle.

THERAPIST:

Yea you have. By the way, that is really good.

(Therapist supports the husband.)

HUSBAND:

Why are you so hung up on me sitting with my legs propped up?

THERAPIST:

Ask her if this feels better.

HUSBAND:

Does this feel better?

(Husband sends a clear message to wife.)

WIFE:

A lot better. It feels nice when you are close to me and look at me because I know you are interested in me.

HUSBAND:

I'm interested in you, but I don't always have time to sit down and you don't always have time to sit down.

WIFE:

Well, we have to make time. Let's make time.

HUSBAND:

When I come home, are you going to stop what you're doing and come in the living room with me and sit down and talk when you are in the kitchen?

(Husband begins to get nervous and the therapist interrupts.)

THERAPIST:

Well, you got him there. What are you going to do with him?

WIFE:

I don't know. I haven't had him there for a long time.

HUSBAND:

Why not?   (Husband attempts to play "tell me why" again.)

WIFE:

Because we are never close like this anymore.

THERAPIST:

Well you are right now. What do you think you could do with him?

WIFE:

[*Laughing*] What could I do with him?   (The interaction between
Make mad, passionate love.   husband and wife becomes quite different from this point on. The dysfunctional process has been interrupted and a different set of interactions starts to develop.)

THERAPIST:

Okay.

WIFE:

No.

THERAPIST:

You don't want to do that?

WIFE:

No, but I'd like to give him a kiss.

[*Kiss*]

WIFE:

It has been a long time.

HUSBAND:

Eight weeks! Is that how long it is?

WIFE:

Poor thing.

HUSBAND:

Poor thing, has it been that long?

WIFE:

I don't know.

THERAPIST:

Do you ever touch her face?

HUSBAND:

Yes.

THERAPIST:

Just kind of . . .

HUSBAND:

What has been happening when I do that? This week when I go to touch you?

WIFE:

Try it again. Try it now.   (Wife tells husband she
                                                         wants to be close.)

HUSBAND:

You like that now. [*Husband touches wife's face.*]

WIFE:

Your hands are hard. [*Says it softly.*]

HUSBAND:

Well, if you want me to touch your face,   (Husband gets nervous.)
you are going to have to go with my hard
hands. They are the only ones I've got.

WIFE:

It's very romantic.

HUSBAND:

Well you have pimples all over your face   (Husband gets nervous.)
and that is not very romantic either. But if
that is the face you got, what am I gonna
do?

THERAPIST:

Well, do you like it?

HUSBAND:

Yes, I like it!

[*Wife laughs.*]

HUSBAND:

That is the only hand I've got.

WIFE:

You can put cream on it.

THERAPIST:

Gee, I am really happy. I feel good right   (Therapist supports the
now.   couple.)

HUSBAND:

You do?

THERAPIST:
> Yea, I really do. I found out that not only can you two talk, but you can actually do a little loving. That is really nice. I've never seen that before.

HUSBAND:
> I'm a man of all . . .

WIFE:
> Jack of all trades.

(Husband and wife are being supportive of each other.)

HUSBAND:
> Jack of all trades.

WIFE:
> He has hidden secrets.

HUSBAND:
> Can I sit back?

WIFE:
> No.

HUSBAND:
> No?

WIFE:
> No.

HUSBAND:
> I didn't sit back, did I?

WIFE:
> Is it uncomfortable sitting that way?

HUSBAND:
> I am leaning forward. You are not leaning forward.

(A much more functional interactional sequence that will allow both husband and wife to meet their needs for intimacy.)

WIFE:
> Do you want me to lean forward?

HUSBAND:
> Yes.

WIFE:
> This is nice.

HUSBAND:
> You like it?

WIFE:

Yea.

HUSBAND:

Then why don't we do this at home?

THERAPIST:

[*To the wife*] Do you feel all cold and
dead inside?

(Wife has complained in
the past about feeling
cold and dead inside.
The therapist wants her
to understand the differ-
ent feeling that results
from a changed interac-
tional sequence.)

WIFE:

No.

[*Laughter*]

HUSBAND:

Do you feel warm inside?

WIFE:

Yes because I am close to you. [*Wife
laughs and starts sobbing.*]

HUSBAND:

What is so funny?

WIFE:

Nothing is funny. [*Crying and laughing*]

HUSBAND:

Why are you laughing? Is that your nervous laugh? What are you doing?

(Husband checks out his
concern. This is very
functional communica-
tion.)

[*Silence. Wife starts to cry heavily.*]

THERAPIST:

What is going on now?

HUSBAND:

What do you feel?

(Again, husband checks
it out.)

[*Silence*]

HUSBAND:

Does my arm smell that bad?

(Husband starts to get
nervous.)

THERAPIST:
> [To wife] Why are you crying?

HUSBAND:
> Do I have such a smelly arm?

[Silence]

HUSBAND:
> It smells? I took a shower last week, what do you mean?

(Husband feels anxious and tries to get his wife to laugh.)

THERAPIST:
> Why are you crying?

WIFE:
> I don't know.

THERAPIST:
> He is getting all nervous and I am too because we don't know why you are crying.

(Therapist checks it out and sends a clear message about how he is feeling.)

WIFE:
> Well, it is because I never feel relaxed enough to feel this way. And I wish I always did . . . it makes me feel good, because you are close. [Crying]

HUSBAND:
> You shouldn't feel bad because you don't always feel this way. You are not crying because you feel good this way. You are crying because you feel good this way today and you didn't feel good like this all the time. [Husband states this very softly with concern.]

(Husband offers his wife support.)

THERAPIST:
> You can put her in your lap if you want.

(Therapist offers another way to be supportive.)

HUSBAND:
> Do you want to sit in my lap? What else do you want me to do?

(Husband checks it out with his wife.)

WIFE:
> I want you to hold me.

(Wife sends a clear message.)

[Silence—husband holds his wife.]

[*Long silence, with low talking.*
Husband holds wife. Wife cries and
husband strokes her.]

(Husband and wife both
share a moment of in-
tense intimacy.)

HUSBAND:

We are producing a gap on the tape.

THERAPIST:

It's a beautiful silence.

(Therapist supports the
couple.)

[*Laughter*]

THERAPIST:

That was nice.

CONCLUSION

After this interview, the couple continued in marital therapy for approximately three months. They continued to improve their relationship and in the one year follow-up, the couple reported that things are
fine.

6

The Morris Family: Working with the Total Family Group

The Morris family, consisting of Bob, the husband, Gerry, the wife, Bev, the daughter, and Agnes, the grandmother, was referred for family therapy after they had consulted with a psychiatrist about Gerry's depression. The psychiatrist did not choose to give the wife medication as he believed the depression to be reactive to the family situation. The referral for family therapy was fully explained to both the husband and the wife, although this couple denied such understanding in the initial family interview. In this initial interview, the family seated itself as in Figure 11.

The seating arrangement reflects a family coalition of husband, daughter, and grandmother against the wife. The wife has difficulty expressing herself within the interview, as the other family members freely interrupt. The wife reinforces the process by not insisting on her right to speak, by covering her anger, and by refusing to ask for support. The therapist's goal in the initial part of the interview is to make contact and form a starting relationship with each member of the family group. Not a great deal of time is spent on assessment, as the primary dysfunctional family process (i.e., the family's unbalanced structure maintained by family interruption) is fairly clear.

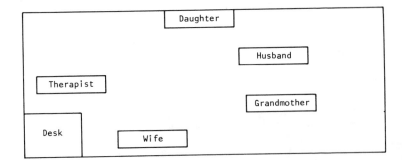

Figure 11.   *The Morris family*

[*Background noise as the family enters the interview room.*]

THERAPIST:
   I'm glad you could make it today. Why   (Structure)
   don't we all have a seat?

DAUGHTER:
   Where should I sit?

THERAPIST:
   Sit where you feel comfortable.   (Structure and emotional
                                               accommodation)

[*Chairs moving—noise*]

THERAPIST:
   Okay, I'm Jim. I'd like to know your   (Structure)
   names.

[*Silence*]

THERAPIST:
   Mr. Morris, could you introduce me to   (Structure)
   the family?

HUSBAND:
   Well, uh . . . this is my mother, Agnes.   (Husband introduces his
                                               mother and daughter be-
                                               fore he introduces his
                                               wife. This often indicates
                                               a family structure prob-
                                               lem.)

THERAPIST:
   [*Shakes hands with grandmother*] Hello,
   how are you?

GRANDMOTHER:
> Hello.

HUSBAND:
> This is my daughter, Bev.

THERAPIST:
> Hi. [*Shakes hands with daughter*]

DAUGHTER:
> Hi.

HUSBAND:
> And this is my wife, Gerry.

THERAPIST:
> Hello. [*Shakes hands with wife*]

WIFE:
> Hi.

THERAPIST:
> Okay. Can I call people by their first names?

(Therapist checks out with the family if this is okay. Models communication and how to check out communication.)

HUSBAND:
> First names are fine.

THERAPIST:
> How about the rest of the family? [*Looks at other family members.*]

[*Family members all nod yes.*]

THERAPIST:
> Okay. I'd like to get to know something about each of you as a person. Can I start with you, Bob?

(Structure)

HUSBAND:
> There's not much to tell.

THERAPIST:
> I'm sure there's a good bit you could tell.

(Emotional accommodation)

HUSBAND:
> Well—I don't know. I'm a school teacher.

THERAPIST:
> A school teacher?

HUSBAND:
> Yes.

THERAPIST:
   What do you teach?
HUSBAND:
   Sixth grade.
THERAPIST:
   Do you enjoy it?
HUSBAND:
   Yea.
THERAPIST:
   Do you feel good about your job and is it   (Therapist models how to
   something you enjoy?   check out the messages a
                                                        person receives.)

HUSBAND:
   I'd say so.
THERAPIST:
   Are you good at your job?
HUSBAND:
   I'm a good teacher.
THERAPIST:
   How long have you been at it?   (Emotional accommoda-
                                                        tion)

HUSBAND:
   About seven years.
THERAPIST:
   Okay. Fine.

[Silence]

THERAPIST:
   How about you, Gerry? Are you a teacher   (Therapist asks questions
   also?   to get the wife talking and
                                                       to express his interest in
                                                       her as a person.)

WIFE:
   I used to be.
THERAPIST:
   Are you working now?
WIFE:
   No . . . just a housewife.
THERAPIST:
   Okay, so now you're a full-time mother   (Therapist relables)
   and wife. Do you enjoy it?
WIFE:
   Well . . . yes.

THERAPIST:

You kind of hesitated. Does that mean you're sometimes not so sure?

(Checks out with wife her incongruent coding operation.)

WIFE:

Well . . . sometimes.

DAUGHTER:

[*Interrupting*] She's not happy.

THERAPIST:

When you were a teacher, what did you teach?

(Asks the wife a question to help her manifest herself.)

WIFE:

English.

THERAPIST:

Okay, any hobbies?

[*Silence*]

WIFE:

Sometimes I play the piano.

THERAPIST:

Okay, fine. Do you enjoy it?

(Emotional accommodation)

WIFE:

Well . . . yea.

THERAPIST:

Okay, fine. Bev, how about you? What can you tell me about yourself?

(Structure and emotional accommodation)

DAUGHTER:

I'm in the eighth grade.

THERAPIST:

Okay.

DAUGHTER:

I like to swim.

THERAPIST:

You do?

DAUGHTER:

Yea.

HUSBAND:

Bev's on the swimming team.

THERAPIST:

You are?

(Emotional accommodation)

DAUGHTER:
> Yea.

THERAPIST:
> [*To grandmother*] How about you? What   (Structure)
> would you tell me about yourself?

GRANDMOTHER:
> Well, I'm retired.

THERAPIST:
> Were you a school teacher too?   (Structure. Therapist
>   uses questions to help the
>   family members manifest
>   themselves. Also shows
>   interest on the part of the
>   therapist.)

GRANDMOTHER:
> No, I was a secretary.

THERAPIST:
> Okay, fine. How long have you been re-
> tired?

GRANDMOTHER:
> About eight years.

THERAPIST:
> How do you spend your time?

GRANDMOTHER:
> Mostly with Bev, plus I . . . I'm in a
> number of clubs.

THERAPIST:
> [*To Bev*] Is she a good grandma?   (Emotional accommoda-
>   tion)

DAUGHTER:
> Yea.

THERAPIST:
> Do you two spend a lot of time together?   (The therapist thinks that
>   the grandmother spends
>   more time with the
>   daughter than the
>   mother and wants infor-
>   mation about this—
>   assessment.)

GRENDMOTHER:
> Yes.

THERAPIST:

> Okay, fine. Anything anybody else wants
> to say?

[*Silence*]

THERAPIST:

> Okay, I'd like to know why you people are
> here today. Why did you people come?

HUSBAND:

> Well . . .

WIFE:

> I'm the only one who should be here, but
> you said on the phone to bring everyone.

(The wife, who seems depressed, wants to grab responsibility for the problem. This is typical in depression.)

THERAPIST:

> Yes, I did. But why do you think you're
> the only one who should be here?

(Therapist asks a question to help wife manifest herself.)

WIFE:

> It's my problem.

THERAPIST:

> What is?

WIFE:

> I'm depressed. I . . .

HUSBAND:

> [*Interrupting*] She's been depressed about
> a year.

(Husband agrees with wife that it's her problem.)

DAUGHTER:

> She's always crying.

(Daughter also agrees that Mom is the patient.)

THERAPIST:

> [*To daughter*] Why do you think she
> cries?

DAUGHTER:

> I don't know.

THERAPIST:

> So ask your mom how come she cries.

(Therapist attempts to facilitate contact between mother and daughter,

and Grandmother inter-
rupts.)

GRANDMOTHER:

It's not Bev's fault.

THERAPIST:

I didn't say it was. I just think if Bev
doesn't know why, she could find out by
asking.

HUSBAND:

Well, it's not Bev's fault.

DAUGHTER:

I didn't do anything.

THERAPIST:

[*To wife*] Everyone in the family protects
Bev, and I didn't even accuse her of anything. Who protects you?

(Therapist comments on
the apparent coalition of
the family against the
wife.)

WIFE:

Well . . .

DAUGHTER:

[*Interrupts*] She doesn't need protection.
She just cries all the time.

(The family manifests a
coalition against the
wife. The way the coali-
tion is maintained is
through interruption.)

THERAPIST:

[*To wife*] Well . . .

WIFE:

I don't . . .

DAUGHTER:

[*Interrupting*] She cries all the time.
She's always upset.

THERAPIST:

Did you notice Bev just interrupted you?
How do you feel when that happens?

(Therapist comments on
the interruption process.)

WIFE:

Well . . .

THERAPIST:

Good, or not too good?

(Therapist attempts to
help wife send a clear
message.)

WIFE:

Well . . .

THERAPIST:

Which?

[*Silence*]

WIFE:

Not too good. I . . .

HUSBAND:

[*Interrupting*] Well, she didn't mean to interrupt. She's just . . .

(Therapist attempt is blocked by the husband's interruption.)

GRANDMOTHER:

She's a good girl.

THERAPIST:

[*To husband*] Did you hear what your wife just said?

(Therapist attempts to instigate interaction between husband and wife.)

[*Silence*]

THERAPIST:

Well?

HUSBAND:

No.

THERAPIST:

Okay, ask her what she said.

WIFE:

[*Tearing up*] Oh nothing.

(The wife demonstrates reciprocity by not speaking when she does have the chance.)

[*Silence*]

THERAPIST:

Sounded like something to me.

[*Husband shrugs shoulders.*]

DAUGHTER:

See, now she's getting upset. She's always crying.

(The family uses the wife's tears to illustrate that the wife is the problem.)

HUSBAND:

She gets like this a lot. We took her to a psychiatrist to get some medicine or something.

THERAPIST:

[*To wife*] Did he give you any medicine?   (The therapist wants to know for assessment. Many times, depressed people are overmedicated.)

WIFE:

No. He said it was a family problem. He sent us to you.

THERAPIST:

What do you think? You think it's a family problem?

WIFE:

[*Softly*] I don't know.

THERAPIST:

Why did he say it was a family problem?   (Assessment)

HUSBAND:

He just said it seemed like a family problem.

THERAPIST:

Well, I see one family problem. People interrupt each other in this family and then people feel unloved. I think Gerry feels unheard a lot of the time and then she gets depressed. Is that right Gerry?

(Therapist comments upon his assessment of what is going on.)
(Checks it out with the wife.)

WIFE:

Well sometimes it's hard to get a word in . . .

(The wife sends an unclear message—sometimes.)

GRANDMOTHER:

[*Interrupting*] But it's not Bev's fault. She's just . . .

(Grandmother blocks the wife's coding operation by interrupting.)

THERAPIST:

[*To grandmother*] Are you aware that you just interrupted Gerry? She was . . .

(The therapist comments on what he sees happening.)

HUSBAND:

>   [*Interrupting*] She didn't mean to.

(Husband continues the family process.)

THERAPIST:

>   Are you aware you just interrupted me?

HUSBAND:

>   No. I'm sorry.

THERAPIST:

>   [*To husband*] Okay, I want you to do yourself and the family a favor. I want you to point out every time someone interrupts your wife. Just ask them if they are aware that they just interrupted Gerry. Okay? Will you do that?

(The therapist attempts to put the husband in a coalition with his wife by giving him an assignment. This should break up the family process and allow a new pattern to emerge. This will set a generational boundary between the parents and the daughter.)

HUSBAND:

>   Well . . .

THERAPIST:

>   Give it a try.

HUSBAND:

>   I don't see what good that will do.

(Husband feels nervous.)

THERAPIST:

>   Ask your wife if she thinks it will help.

(Having the husband ask this question puts him into contact with his wife.)

HUSBAND:

>   Well . . .

THERAPIST:

>   Go on, ask her.

HUSBAND:

>   [*To wife*] Will that help?

(Husband communicates directly with his wife.)

WIFE:

>   I . . . I don't know, maybe.

(Wife demonstrates reciprocity.)

THERAPIST:

>   [*To wife*] You enjoy being interrupted?

(Therapist confronts wife.)

[*Silence*]

WIFE:

No.

THERAPIST:

Well, how come it won't help?

[*Silence*]

THERAPIST:

Well?

WIFE:

Yea, it would help.   (Wife sends a clear message.)

THERAPIST:

Okay, so tell your husband it will help.
Look at him and tell him.

WIFE:

[*To husband*] That would help. It . . .   (The wife sends a clear message to her husband and the daughter interrupts.)

DAUGHTER:

[*Interrupting*] This is crazy.

[*Silence*]

DAUGHTER:

Well, it is.

THERAPIST:

[*To husband*] Bob, I think you just missed   (Therapist reminds the husband of his assignment.)
one.

[*Silence*]

HUSBAND:

Okay, Bev are you aware that you just
interrupted your mother?

DAUGHTER:

Okay, but it is.

THERAPIST:

Okay, Gerry, go on and finish what you   (Therapist helps the wife with her coding to husband.)
were saying.

WIFE:

I think it would help.

(Wife sends a clear message and is looking less depressed.)

THERAPIST:

Why? Why do you think it would help?

WIFE:

I never seem to be able to say anything or have anyone listen . . .

GRANDMOTHER:

[Interrupting] That's not right.

(Grandmother continues the process.)

THERAPIST:

Bob?

(Therapist reminds the husband of his assignment, and as a result, the husband is being supportive of his wife.)

HUSBAND:

[To grandmother] Mother, are you aware that you just interrupted Gerry?

THERAPIST:

Good. Okay, tell your wife you wanted to hear what she was saying.

(Therapist tells husband to check it out.)

HUSBAND:

[To wife] What were you saying?

(Husband asks wife for clarification and his wife sends a clear message.)

WIFE:

I just don't feel like anyone in the family listens to me.

THERAPIST:

And when you're being interrupted, do you get the idea that they don't care about you?

(The therapist checks out with the wife his evaluation of the real issue.)

[Silence]

THERAPIST:

Well?

WIFE:

[Tearing up] Sometimes.

(Wife sends an unclear message.)

THERAPIST:
Well, do you think that has anything to do with getting depressed? I do.

WIFE:
I don't know. Maybe.

THERAPIST:
Well, do you feel as depressed when your husband tells people they're interrupting? Do you feel depressed then?

(Therapist confronts wife.)

WIFE:
[Smiling] No . . . No I don't.

(Wife sends a clear message.)

DAUGHTER:
[Interrupting] This is crazy.

(The daughter and grandmother continue the interruption process.)

GRANDMOTHER:
I don't understand this at all.

[Grandmother and Bev both talk at once.]

HUSBAND:
Bev, are you aware that you just interrupted?

(The husoand supports his wife.)

THERAPIST:
Good.

(Therapist thanks the husband.)

DAUGHTER:
I don't understand this.

(Daughter asks for clarification.)

THERAPIST:
When people interrupt your mom, she thinks you don't care about her and don't want to listen to her.

GRANDMOTHER:
Why are you picking on her? She's not a bad girl.

THERAPIST:
I know. She just interrupts sometimes.

WIFE:
She's not bad. I just wish she'd stop interrupting.

(The wife defends the daughter.)

THERAPIST:

    So you kind of like her. You have a good feeling about Bev most of the time.

WIFE:

    Yea.

THERAPIST:

    Do you take time with her? Listen to her, like most daughters and mother?

WIFE:

    I used to, but lately, not a lot. I . . . I've felt bad, and haven't done it.

[Silence]

DAUGHTER:

    [Tearing up] She . . . She's not like she used to be. She used to take time.

(The daughter sends an unclear message.)

THERAPIST:

    [Softly] So you'd like some of Mom's attention.

(Therapist helps the daughter code her message in a clear way.)

DAUGHTER:

    [Crying] Yes.

THERAPIST:

    So . . .

GRANDMOTHER:

    [Interrupting] See? She's upset.

(Grandmother interrupts.)

THERAPIST:

    [To daughter] Tell your mom that. Tell her you want some of her attention.

[Daughter crying]

DAUGHTER:

    [Softly] Yes.

(The daughter admits she wants attention.)

THERAPIST:

    Is that why you interrupt?

DAUGHTER:

    [Crying] Yes.

WIFE:

    [Tearing up] I . . . I don't . . . know what . . .

THERAPIST:
>   [*To wife*] Ask her what would help.

(Therapist helps the wife find out what would help.)

WIFE:
>   [*To daughter*] What would help, Bev?

[*Silence*]

DAUGHTER:
>   Nothing.

THERAPIST:
>   Bev, tell her what would help.

(Therapist supports the daughter.)

[*Daughter crying*]

DAUGHTER:
>   Sit next to me.

(Daughter sends a clear message and mother responds.)

[*Gerry moves over and puts her arm around Bev. Both mother and daughter cry.*]

[*Long silence*]

WIFE:
>   [*To therapist*] It's been a long time since I've felt like a parent.

(Both the wife and the daughter feel better as they are meeting their needs for intimacy)

THERAPIST:
>   You seem to do pretty well.

[*Daughter and mother both laugh.*]

THERAPIST:
>   That's nice.

(Therapist supports wife and daughter.)

[*Silence*]

THERAPIST:
>   You know, I don't think this would have happened without Bob's help. I'd like to see you tell him thanks for not letting Bev interrupt.

(Therapist points out the husband's contribution to the improved outcome.)

WIFE:

> That's right.

THERAPIST:

> Tell him it felt good.

WIFE:

> [To husband] Thanks.

(Wife sends husband a clear message.)

[Husband acts nervous, moves, fidgets, and gets out a cigarette. Therapist offers husband a light.]

(The husband is apparently not used to receiving thanks. The therapist supports the husband.)

HUSBAND:

> [To therapist] I don't understand what happened.

THERAPIST:

> You supported your wife. She felt better and could give Bev some attention.

(The therapist gives a clear answer.)

[Silence]

THERAPIST:

> [To husband] Have you and your wife been supporting each other lately?

HUSBAND:

> Not really.

THERAPIST:

> So things haven't been real good for you either?

(The therapist helps the husband send a clear message about how he is feeling and what he would like to happen differently in the family.)

HUSBAND:

> [Softly] That's right.

THERAPIST:

> Is that a situation you'd like to work on? It seemed to help Gerry quite a bit when you supported her. I mean, she looks a lot less depressed to me.

HUSBAND:

> [Laughs] Yea, she does.

THERAPIST:

[*To wife*] I'm not just making that up, am I?

WIFE:

[*Laughing*] No.

THERAPIST:

[*To husband*] So you want to work with Gerry about supporting each other more often?

HUSBAND:

[*Smiles*] Yes. I'd like that.

(Husband sends a clear message.)

THERAPIST:

[*To grandmother*] What about you? You think Gerry looks any better right now?

(The therapist has not spent enough time with the grandmother and wants to include her to a greater degree.)

GRANDMOTHER:

Yes, and Bev feels better too.

THERAPIST:

Yea, she does.

[*Daughter laughs.*]

THERAPIST:

[*To the whole family*] Well, it seems to me that it would be good to see the whole family every other week, and Gerry and Bob alone in between. I think that this would be the best approach. What do you people think?

(The therapist starts to develop a contract. This occurs after the family has experienced an interactional change. A contract can now be made that is a family contract rather than an individual contract.)

HUSBAND:

Sounds good to me.

WIFE:

Yea.

DAUGHTER:

Okay.

[*Silence*]

THERAPIST:

[To grandmother] How about you?

GRANDMOTHER:

Well . . .

THERAPIST:

I think you are an important part of the family. You and Bev have a great relationship and I think it would help quite a bit if you come.

(Therapist sends the grandmother a clear message saying he feels it is important for her to come.)

GRANDMOTHER:

Well . . .

DAUGHTER:

Grandma!

(Daughter requests the grandmother's presence.)

THERAPIST:

See!

GRANDMOTHER:

Okay. [Laughs]

THERAPIST:

Good. I'm glad.

[Silence]

THERAPIST:

Okay. I'd like to spend a little time with Bob and Gerry. Then I'll see the rest of you in two weeks, okay?

(Therapist wants to work with the marital pair to reinforce the boundary change that has occurred within the interview. This separation reinforces the marital couple as a family subsystem.)

DAUGHTER:

Okay.

THERAPIST:

[Stands up and shakes hands with daughter] It's been nice meeting you, Bev.

[Daughter laughs.]

THERAPIST:

> [*Shakes hands with grandmother*] I'll see you in two weeks. Thanks for coming. Okay?

(Emotional accommodation)

GRANDMOTHER:

> Okay. See you in two weeks.

[*Grandmother and daughter leave the room.*]

THERAPIST:

> Okay, why don't the two of you change around a bit so you can sit next to each other.

(The therapist wants to facilitate more contact between the marital pair and requests a physical seating arrangement change.)

[*Husband and wife move chairs.*]

THERAPIST:

> Okay, Bob, you said earlier that you felt you and Gerry haven't been as close to each other recently.

(Therapist restates the husband's previous message about wanting to be closer to his wife.)

HUSBAND:

> Yea.

THERAPIST:

> So you'd like to work on being closer to your wife?

HUSBAND:

> Yea, I'd like to do that, but I'm not sure how.

(Husband sends a clear message.)

THERAPIST:

> Okay, well, one thing that you did today that seemed to work was to try and keep from interrupting. You know, spend more time trying to listen.

(Therapist helps the husband focus on a change that worked and can be repeated.)

HUSBAND:

> Yea, that did seem to work.

(The couple is showing good affect. The wife is not depressed and the husband feels less nervous.)

THERAPIST:
Yes, it seemed to help get to know her a
little better.

[*Wife laughs; husband smiles.*]

THERAPIST:
So far, at least, as a start, you'll try to
support your wife by listening and letting
people know when they're interrupting.

(Therapist clarifies what
he wants to happen and
what he believes is the
agreement.)

HUSBAND:
Yea, okay.

THERAPIST:
How about you, Gerry? What would you
be willing to work on?

(The therapist asks the
wife to tell what she is
willing to change and do
differently.)

WIFE:
I'm not sure.

(Wife sends a clear mes-
sage.)

THERAPIST:
Well, ask Bob what you did today that was
different and he enjoyed.

(Tells wife to check it out
with her husband.)

WIFE:
What did I do differently?

(Wife sends a clear mes-
sage.)

HUSBAND:
You talked more.

THERAPIST:
You mattered.

(Emotional accommoda-
tion)

HUSBAND:
[*Laughs*] Yea.

THERAPIST:
So you want her to talk to you more. You
want some attention, too.

(Therapist helps the hus-
band send a clear mes-
sage.)

HUSBAND:
That would be nice.

THERAPIST:
One of the things I notice, Gerry, is that
when you feel bad, you sit by yourself and

(Therapist openly tells
the wife how he sees her

don't say anything. Nobody knows how to help and your husband begins to feel pretty alone too when you do that.

(send unclear messages which lead to confusion and distance.)

WIFE:

Well . . .

THERAPIST:

Hell, he loses a wife. I mean, he might like some attention too.

WIFE:

Well, when I feel bad I just don't want to . . .

(Wife is not sure she wants to change.)

THERAPIST:

Ask?

WIFE:

Yea.

THERAPIST:

That's noble.

(Therapist confronts wife.)

WIFE:

[Angry] What do you mean?

THERAPIST:

Have you ever asked him what he wants?

WIFE:

Well . . . no.

THERAPIST:

Why not?

WIFE:

I guess I think he doesn't want to be bothered.

(The wife is explicit about how she evaluates her husband's distance.)

THERAPIST:

A noble mind reader at that.

[Wife laughs.]

THERAPIST:

That seems sad to me.

[Silence]

WIFE:

I . . . I will work on that. I'll talk to him.

THERAPIST:

Well, maybe I'm a mind reader, too. Maybe you should check it out with him. Don't take my word for it.

WIFE:

> [*To husband*] Would you like that better?

(Wife sends a clear message.)

HUSBAND:

> [*Softly*] Yes.

(The husband sends a clear message. His nonverbal tone is congruent with his verbal "yes.")

THERAPIST:

> Okay, fine. Now at least we all know.

[*Silence*]

THERAPIST:

> How much time do you two spend together?

WIFE:

> Not much. We used to spend time together, but we stopped.

THERAPIST:

> Is that right, Bob?

HUSBAND:

> Yea. I just . . . She got depressed and I . . . I just avoided the situation, so to speak.

(This could easily turn into a "who done it" game.)

WIFE:

> I got depressed after you started working extra . . .

THERAPIST:

> I'm not sure it's important how it started. What seems important is that you both are saying you want to change it.

(The therapist interrupts this, as it will lead nowhere.)

HUSBAND:

> Yea . . . that's right.

THERAPIST:

> How much time together this week do you two think you could tolerate?

(The therapist is aware that the couple has made a change. Change is generally somewhat frightening and the therapist predicts the fear response.)

HUSBAND:

> Tolerate? That's what I want.

THERAPIST:

It might be difficult. You're both used to being apart. You might get nervous.

WIFE:

[*Laughing*] No.

THERAPIST:

Okay, let's see. Move your chairs real close facing each other. Okay, and look at each other.

(The therapist sets up an even more intimate situation to help the couple feel closer and to experience the anxiety associated with change.)

WIFE:

[*Laughs*]

HUSBAND:

It's different.

THERAPIST:

Kind of nervous?

HUSBAND:

A little. [*Husband holds wife's hand.*]

HUSBAND:

It's okay.

WIFE:

It's nice.

THERAPIST:

Okay, but a little nervous?

WIFE:

Yes!

THERAPIST:

Okay, look, what I'd like you to do this week is find at least an hour every other day and spend it just with each other. Okay? Go out to dinner, take a walk, I don't care, just plan on an hour, okay?

(The therapist gives a homework assignment that includes (1) more intimacy and closeness between husband and wife and (2) a way of helping them both handle any anxiety that may occur as a result of the closeness.)

[*Husband and wife both nod yes.*]

THERAPIST:

Then write on a piece of paper what you're thinking and any feelings you

(This will help the couple handle any anxi-

have. Then bring it with you next week. Okay?

ety associated with the closeness. It will also be useful to talk about it in the next session.)

[*Silence*]

THERAPIST:

Okay? Are you willing to do this?

HUSBAND:

Sure.

WIFE:

Okay.

THERAPIST:

Fine. Okay, why don't we stop for today and I'll see you two next week. Same time?

(Therapist ends the session.)

HUSBAND:

Fine, thanks.

THERAPIST:

Okay.

[*Therapist shakes hands with both husband and wife and the couple leaves.*]

The Morris family was seen eleven times as a total group, and the husband and wife were seen alone on five different occasions. The family made good progress. Gerry's depression cleared up and has not returned. Bev is now a senior in high school and Agnes still lives with the family. The parents report an improved marital relationship and the family as a whole considers their experience in family therapy extremely helpful.

7

Grief Work:
A Family Approach

Family therapy is different from individual therapy in that a primary goal in the family approach is to help the members of the family group improve and develop a better relationship with each other rather than with the therapist. The individual therapist sees the development of a positive relationship between worker and client as a primary curative factor. The family therapist sees the development of a positive relationship between the worker and the family not as a primary curative factor but rather as one means to an end, namely the development of improved communication within the total family group.

Although much has been written about the value of worker empathy and understanding in the successful resolution of grief, it is the author's opinion that unless such a therapeutic relationship helps the grieving client receive the same understanding from the family as from the therapist, it may lead to serious family relationship problems in the future. The purpose of this chapter is to illustrate the point that the very factors traditionally thought of as curative in the individual therapy relationship, when applied to the process of grief can include a destructive element, namely the distancing of the grieving individual from a major source of "continued" support, his or her own natural family group. In addition, the author will recommend a specific approach to family grief work that he believes does not include the previously mentioned destructive element of the individual approach.

MR. AND MRS. KROFT

Mr. and Mrs. Kroft requested marital counseling recognizing that their relationship had deteriorated in the "past few years." Within the initial conjoint interview, the Kroft's exhibited an avoid-avoid relationship style that included both indirect communication as well as incongruent manifestation of self. Mrs. Kroft stated that she had been in therapy the prior two years after she became depressed over the death of her son. She felt as though her previous therapist was one of the "kindest people alive." Mr. Kroft stated that he had been very upset about the death of his son but had not requested therapy as he felt "capable of handling the problem himself." Mrs. Kroft felt she had developed a number of helpful insights as a result of her previous therapy and stated that her therapist had been very supportive.

An Analysis of the Case

In the author's opinion, the previous therapist had done an excellent job. She had been able to get through Mrs. Kroft's symptoms and make contact. She had facilitated a good working relationship, had helped Mrs. Kroft develop a number of new coping skills and had provided support in a nonsmothering, appropriate way. As a result, Mrs. Kroft was able to resolve her grief. Yet something went wrong. Mrs. Kroft received understanding and support from her therapist, not her husband. The husband was not included as he did not express a "personal need." Intimacy was shared between the grieving client and the therapist. This process excluded the husband as a person who "could help."

As helpers, we attempt to develop our capacity for understanding, empathy, and open communication. Often we become quite skilled. Yet in many instances this very skill that we have so carefully developed excludes those individuals in our client's natural environment who could also help. We can become a hard act to follow. This is what happened with Mr. and Mrs. Kroft. The therapist's "achievement" excluded Mr. Kroft's opportunity to support his wife in a time of need.

The wife was unable to see her husband as supportive because he could not "measure up" to the previous therapist's skill. The husband, a person who tended to distance himself in times of emotional stress, was not provided the opportunity to learn new relationship skills that could be developed by both husband and wife, into a deeper, more intimate marriage. The therapist's skill, used successfully to help Mrs. Kroft resolve her grief, also resulted in additional distance between husband and wife, which grew over a period of time. It is unfortunate that the therapist's skill had not been used to encourage the "husband's help."

As has been noted in the first three chapters, family and marital communication includes family coding, family decoding, family structure, and family reciprocity. Without functional communication rules, the family will be unable to provide for the psychological needs of its members.

In the Kroft illustration, the therapist's interventions can be understood as functioning in a way that blocked family communications. The therapist's interventions helped prevent Mrs. Kroft from sending clear coding messages to her husband (she was sending them to the therapist) and also allowed Mr. Kroft a great opportunity to distort (in his thoughts and feelings) the lack of contact from his wife. This approach also did not facilitate a process of checking things out between husband and wife, and emotional distance between the couple was reinforced. Again, the very qualities that made the previous therapist effective in helping Mrs. Kroft resolve her grief, helped promote distance between the husband and wife. This therapy situation is illustrated in Figure 12.

FAMILY GRIEF WORK

The author has found it helpful to view family grief work as a method aimed at mobilizing and developing the natural curative properties inherent in the family group. The method follows the stages suggested by Greenberg (1975), which are (1) announcement, (2) acknowledgment, (3) mourning, and (4) renewal, and includes the advantage of

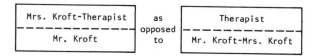

Figure 12. *The Kroft therapy situation.*

preventing many future family communication problems by reinforcing family relatedness and family coping skills.

Family Announcement

Family announcement is a telling of the death (Greenberg, 1975).
Such a telling needs to occur in an experiential way that includes
emotional recall of significant details along with the realization of a
significant loss (Greenberg, 1975). It is often found that the family
group will attempt to silence family members who wish to openly
manifest thoughts and feelings about the loss. The family's loss creates
stress and the family may attempt to impose limits upon what can
openly be talked about. This restriction upon coding is based upon the
myth that any open acknowledgment of the death is a dangerous thing.
The family as a group will cooperate to maintain the myth.

In the family approach to the resolution of grief, the family
therapist counters the family myth. Within the conjoint family interview the therapist violates the family silence rule by feeling free to
comment on anything he feels, sees, hears, or does not understand
(Andrews, 1974). The family therapist feels free to announce the death
by asking all family members to comment about their understanding of
the death and to allow each other some understanding of each person's
resulting emotional state. The myth must be countered as family avoidance leaves each member up in the air, confused and distant from
each other in a time when they especially need each other's support.
The therapy goal in this stage is to facilitate from all family member
an announcement about the death and a more open expression of self.

Family Acknowledgment

Family acknowledgment is the realization by all family members that
the loss cannot be changed (Greenberg, 1975). Unless such a realization occurs, the family will not understand the meaning of the death
announcement and will not enter into the stage of mourning. The lack
of acknowledgment is again a form of family denial which will initially
avoid pain but may later result in family distance as well as the development of symptoms. The family therapist again counters this process by asking each family member to tell his or her experience of the
death and what it means to them. Such expression when witnessed by
the total family group counters isolation. Each family member is engaged in a process of sharing each other's pain.

Family Mourning

Family mourning is the direct sharing and manifestation of feelings among all members of the family group. Each family member is provided the opportunity of telling (as well as being heard by) the other family members how the experience has affected him. Similarities of expression are recognized and the family begins to experience a closeness based upon mutual empathy and a recognition of each other's pain. The family members begin to know each other within the context of the death. The process of hearing and telling each other provides an experience of family intimacy and trust which then can be generalized for future family problems and concerns.

Family Renewal

Family renewal is a process in which the members of the family group, having announced, acknowledged, and mourned the death, search and find alternative ways of meeting psychological needs that do not depend on the presence of the deceased (Greenberg, 1975). This process can only occur in an atmosphere in which the family membes feel free to talk openly about their needs and what they each feel able to give to others. The renewal process depends to a large extent upon the level of sharing that has occurred in the three previous stages. If the family members have used the event of death to inhibit family communication, such negotiation will not occur. If the family has been helped to speak and hear, the process of renewal may result in a level of family functioning that is even greater than that prior to the death. In the renewal stage, again the therapist's goal is to facilitate listening and expression from all members of the family group. In addition, the therapist helps the family group negotiate for joint relationship outcomes.

THE DUMONT FAMILY

The Dumont family (mother, Mary; 14-year-old daughter, Susan; and 8-year-old son, Bobby) requested family therapy because Susan had been running away from home. The running away started six months after her father's death. In the initial conjoint family session, it was found that the daughter ran away from home because she "can't stand to see mother drunk." The son was having stomach problems and the mother stated that she drank to "feel better." The total family seemed depressed. There had been little family discussion of the father's death and the family depression seemed reactive to unresolved family grief. The following transcript segment of the sixteenth family session is presented to illustrate a family that is engaged in the family renewal stage:

THERAPIST:

So what concerns do you people want to share with each other today?

MOTHER:

[*To therapist*] I'm . . . I'm having trouble not drinking again.

THERAPIST:

Okay, so tell your family what goes on with you when that happens.

MOTHER:

[*To children*] Mostly when I get home from work, I get home and you get home from school. I'm tired and you want to show me your papers or ask can you go somewhere. I . . . I'm tired and I want a drink.

THERAPIST:

And when your husband was there, you didn't work, you weren't so tired? It wasn't a problem then?

MOTHER:

Yea . . . but it's different now.

THERAPIST:

[*To children*] You got any ideas?

DAUGHTER:

We could not talk to her when she just comes home.

THERAPIST:

Okay, so check it out. Ask her if that might help?

The family was able to come up with a number of different plans. The following week the family experimented to see which plan worked best. The family's ability to solve this problem resulted from the increased understanding shown between family members which came from the family's communication about the father's death.

SUMMARY

The author has presented the concept of grief as a family issue. Individual approaches to the resolution of grief may result in serious family relationship problems as the individual therapy process may inadvertently block family communication. The successful resolution of grief follows the stages of family announcement, family acknowledgment, family mourning, and family renewal. The therapist's role is to facilitate an open expression of thoughts and feelings between family members in order to stimulate the natural curative processes inherent in the family group.

8

Decreasing Somatic and Physical Complaints

In January, February, and March of 1975, this author received six service requests from individuals who had been referred for counseling by their family physician. The reason for all six referrals was that the referring physician felt that the individual referred was exacerbating physical and somatic complaints through his or her emotional difficulties and that most of the complaints were a direct result of unresolved emotional problems. In view of the fact that all six service requests were similar in the sense that the referring physician hoped that the client would be able to reduce somatic suffering through the counseling process, the author felt it would be interesting to measure the rate of somatic complaints of each individual's family group before, during, and after family therapy. The objective measures used were (1) the amount of money spent on medication by the family and (2) the number of visits to a doctor by family members during the year. Accurate data on the two measures were obtained from the referring physician and each family by reviewing financial records and statements for the years 1974 (pretherapy), 1975 (during therapy), and 1976 (after therapy).

EMOTIONAL PROBLEMS AND SOMATIC COMPLAINTS: A FAMILY VIEW

It has been the author's practice to view many, if not most, somatic complaints as a signal of family dysfunction. This does not mean that somatic complaints should not be checked out by medical evaluation. The author uses a family process transactional framework that focuses upon the areas of (1) family coding operations, (2) family decoding operations, and (3) family structural balance (Lantz, 1977). The framework considers both dyadic and triadic processes and views somatic complaints as often being the logical result whenever the family group is (1) unable to produce clear, precise, and congruent coding behaviors (2) unable to make accurate decoding evaluations of the messages they receive, and (3) unable to develop a balanced family structure in which the parents together give direction to the rest of the family group. This circular family process is illustrated in Figure 13.

A Description of the Six Family Groups

All six family groups came to the attention of this author through a referral from the same family physician. All six families can be described as lower middle class. At least one parental family member in each family group was working. Two of the families (family C and family F) received partial assistance in the form of food stamps and help with medical expenses from the local welfare department. Five of the families were intact. One family (family C) did not include a husband and father, as he had died in an auto accident. All of the families seemed to experience difficulty expressing feelings to each other in the context of the conjoint family interview. The author

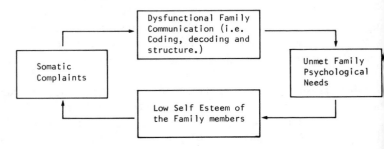

Figure 13. *Family somatic circle.*

experienced each family group as having difficulty experiencing and expressing differences as a positive quality and process. Table 1 lists the family membership of each family group, the money spent on medications during 1974 (an average of $116.08 per individual), the number of visits to the family doctor during 1974 (an average of 12.04 visits per individual), comments on each family group and the source of the families' income during the year (1974) preceding their involvement in family therapy. Note that medication expenses and the number of visits to a doctor for each family group is rather high.

TREATMENT APPROACH

The treatment approach used with each family group was geared toward helping the entire family improve its coding, decoding, and structural family processes in the hope that such an improvement would decrease family emotional pain and the resulting somatic complaints. Efforts were directed at helping the family members work through the five processes of living together presented by Satir (1965), which are (1) manifesting self, (2) separating self from others, (3) making room for self and other, (4) acknowledging differences, and (5) negotiating for joint relationship outcomes. This approach is experiential in the sense that the family members are asked to (1) speak with each other (as opposed to with the therapist) about their concerns, and (2) work out with each other ways of communicating within the conjoint family interview that would be more effective, efficient, and beneficial for all. The therapist's role is to facilitate, redirect, and process family interactions as they occur within the conjoint family interview (Lantz, 1977).

STRUCTURING THE INITIAL FAMILY INTERVIEW

Upon receiving a service request, the author requested by phone that the referred individual bring to the initial interview all members of his or her family presently living at home. It was explained that the author finds this the best way to work and that a further explanation would be provided in the initial session.

In the initial session, the author explained to the family members that _____ (whoever had been referred) had been asked by the family's physician to attend counseling in the hopes that counseling could help decrease any physical complaints that have been

Table 1

| FAMILY MEMBERSHIP | AGE | MONEY SPENT ON MEDICATION 1974 | | VISITS TO A DOCTOR 1974 | | SOURCE OF FAMILY INCOME | COMMENTS (THE IDENTIFIED PATIENT) |
		TOTAL ($)	AVG. ($)	TOTAL	AVG.		
Family A		568	113.60	50	10.0	Father works full time	Mother referred for therapy
Father	42						
Mother	39						
Daughter	18						
Daughter	15						
Son	11						
Family B		418	139.33	34	11.3	Father full time, Mother part time	Mother referred for therapy
Father	33						
Mother	32						
Son	10						
Family C		464	154.66	58	19.3	Mother full time, plus partial assistance	Son referred for therapy
Father	(deceased)						
Mother	36						
Son	14						
Daughter	13						

Family / Member	Age					Employment	Referral
Family D		553	110.60	54	10.8	Father full time, Mother part time	Mother referred for therapy
Father	44						
Mother	45						
Son	19						
Son	17						
Daughter	14						
Family E		604	151.00	66	16.5	Father full time	Father referred for therapy
Father	26						
Mother	22						
Daughter	4						
Daughter	2						
Family F		411	68.50	51	8.5	Father full time, plus partial assistance	Oldest daughter referred for therapy
Father	38						
Mother	38						
Daughter	17						
Son	16						
Daughter	11						
Daughter	5						
Totals 6 Families 26 Individuals		3018	116.08	313	12.04	At least one parent working per family	3 mothers, 1 father, 2 children referred for therapy

brought on by "nerves" and "tension." It was further explained that the author had found it best to work with the whole family in such situations and that the whole family could be of help by being as honest as possible about any concerns, problems, or tensions that they are experiencing in their family life. After a brief discussion of any questions that are asked, the author asks the family membership to be silent and spend about five minutes thinking about "your present concerns" and about "who you most want to tell about your concerns." After the period of silence, the family members are asked to talk with each other about their concerns. The therapist then pulls back from the interaction to watch and assess the family's communication processes.

CHANGE IN THE RATE OF FAMILY SOMATIC COMPLAINTS

Change in the rate of family somatic complaints as measured by money spent on medication and visits to the family physician occurred in all six family groups. The total amount of money spent on medication changed from $3,018.00 (pretherapy) in 1974 to $2,240.00 (during therapy) in 1975, and to $1,682.00 (after therapy) in 1976. A total savings of $2,114.00 for the six families is computed by subtracting the total expenditures of 1975 and 1976 from the 1974 level and by then adding together the 1975 and 1976 savings. All six families decreased their expenditures for medication in 1975 and five of the families continued to reduce medication expenditures in 1976. This is even more remarkable when one remembers that inflation during 1975 and 1976 increased the price of most medications. Total visits to the doctor in 1974 were 313 visits for all the individuals in the six families. This figure was reduced to 225 visits in 1975 (during therapy) and continued to decrease to 166 visits in 1976. Again, all six families reduced visits to the doctor in 1975, and five of the six families reduced such visits in 1976. Total visits saved in 1975 and 1976 were 235 visits. Table 2 provides and compares the data on all six families for the years 1974, 1975, and 1976. It is the author's opinion that the data strongly indicate that family therapy was extremely useful in decreasing family somatic complaints.

LIMITATIONS OF THE DATA

The data provided are descriptive in nature and do not represent a controlled experimental design. Therefore, it is possible (although highly unlikely) that the families would have decreased their medica-

Table 2

	PRETHERAPY 1974		DURING THERAPY 1975		POST-THERAPY 1976	
	TOTAL	AVG.	TOTAL	AVG.	TOTAL	AVG.
Money Spent on Medication						
Family A	$568	$113.60	$413	$ 82.60	$375	$ 75.00
Family B	418	139.33	325	108.33	217	72.33
Family C	464	154.66	316	105.33	326	108.66
Family D	553	110.60	401	80.20	275	55.00
Family E	604	151.00	482	120.50	295	73.75
Family F	411	68.50	303	50.60	194	32.33
Totals and amount per family member	$3,018	$116.08	$2,240	$ 86.15	$1,682	$ 64.69
Visits to a Doctor						
Family A	50	10.0	36	7.2	22	4.2
Family B	34	11.3	24	8.0	18	3.6
Family C	58	19.3	39	13.0	41	13.7
Family D	54	10.8	52	10.2	30	6.0
Family E	66	16.5	41	10.2	31	7.7
Family F	51	8.5	33	5.5	24	4.0
Totals and amount per family member	313	12.1	225	8.7	166	6.1

tion expenditures and visits to their family doctor even without conjoint family therapy. Another limitation of the data is that they do not compare conjoint family therapy with other forms of therapy. Therefore one cannot assume that the change during and after conjoint family therapy is any greater than might have been experienced if the author had used an individual approach. Another limitation is that the data do not control for the referring physician's behavior toward each family group. It is possible that the decrease in medication expenditures was a result of the family physician's refusal to prescribe at previous levels. Also it is possible that the family physician made it more difficult for the family members to make an appointment. Although this variable is not controlled, the author did speak to the referring physician about this possibility and its effects upon the data. The referring physician did not believe that he had changed his approach with any of the family members and felt that family therapy had been of great benefit to all of the patients he had referred.

SUMMARY

Six families in which an individual had been referred for counseling were rated on their level of family somatic complaints. Measures used were the families' expenditures on medication and the number of visits to the family doctor by all individuals in the family group. In the year preceding involvement in conjoint family therapy, the total expenditures for medication by all six family groups was $3,018.00 and the total number of visits to the family doctor by all family members was 313. During the year that the families were involved in therapy, expenditures decreased to $2,240.00 and visits to 225. In the year following therapy, a further reduction was noted to $1,682.00 and 166 visits. The data suggest that conjoint family therapy did help decrease family somatic complaints and resulted in a significant savings of both time and money for all six family groups.

9

Family Therapy and the Beginning Practitioner: One Training Approach

The purpose of this chapter is to present a format for the training of beginning practitioners in family and marital therapy. The advantages of this format include the following: (1) it can easily be integrated into a variety of academic and staff development programs; (2) it takes only two hours per week over a thirty week period; (3) it stresses doing and experimental learning; (4) it provides immediate feedback accompanied by peer support; (5) it provides a solid base for further training where such training opportunities exist; and (6) according to feedback received, it provides for the trainee a set of beginning skills that work and can be applied to a wide variety of practice settings and clinical situations. The format has been used with M.S. degree candidates in psychiatric nursing and M.S.W. degree candidates at Ohio State University, sponsored by the Ohio State University graduate school of nursing. A modified version of the format has been used to train caseworkers at a number of social service agencies in the central Ohio region. Although the format is less intense and aims for different goals, it is patterned to a degree after the first-year training program in conjoint family therapy developed by Andrews (1974) at the Family Institute in Cincinnati, Ohio.

THE FIRST TEN WEEKS: A TRANSACTIONAL AWARENESS GROUP

During the first ten weeks of the program, from eight to twelve trainees are involved in a transactional awareness group. The goals of this group include (1) helping the participants begin to identify and challenge personal transactional patterns that the participants use to prevent themselves from meeting their own psychological needs; (2) having the trainees experience therapists who use a transactional orientation in their leadership approach; (3) helping the trainees realize on an experiential level, the benefits of functional communication; (4) helping the trainees develop empathy and caring for each other; and (5) helping the trainees become more comfortable giving each other negative and positive feedback.

The group generally takes place in a room private enough so that there will be few interruptions. The leader makes sure that there are enough chairs and that ash trays are provided. The author had led this type of group both with and without a co-leader. However, it is the author's preference to work with a co-leader of the opposite sex.*

Initially, the leader(s) tell the group that the purpose of the group and the leader is to help the members become more aware of the benefits of functional communication, to help them identify and change some of their own dysfunctional communication transactions, and to help them realize on a gut level the results of both functional and dysfunctional communication. The participants are told that the leader will attempt to keep the group's focus upon what is happening within and during the group. The leader suggests that the participants read Satir's book, *Conjoint Family Therapy* (Satir, 1964), and Andrews' article, "Identify Maintenance Operations and Group Therapy Process" (Andrews, 1965). Both readings are helpful in understanding communication processes in the group.

The Group Gets Started

After the leaders' initial presentation, the participants are asked to break up into groups of three. They are requested to let the other

*Bev Lenahan, R.N., M.S., Southwest Community Mental Health Center, Columbus, Ohio has been the co-leader in the program at The Ohio State University School of Nursing and has had equal input into the designing of the training program.

members of their small group know something about themselves as a person, i.e., something that has nothing to do with their role of student or helping professional. The participants are asked to concentrate on how they and the other members of the small group manifest themselves and to be aware of how they are feeling as they encounter each other in the small group situation. As this is going on, the leader will observe and make a beginning assessment of the primary transactional style of each group member. The three person group structure provides the participants a situation in which the group members are confronted with the fact that only two members can relate together at any given moment. Some group members will handle this situation by crossing out self for the other ($-S+O$), some will cross out the other for self ($+S-O$), some will cross out both self and other ($-S-O$), and some group members will cross out neither self nor other ($+S+O$).

After approximately fifteen minutes, the leader interrupts the experience and asks the total group to reform in a circle. The members are asked to share with each other what they have experienced or learned about both themselves and fellow members of their small group. The leader offers his observations and, in most instances, this discussion leads to the development of confrontation and support within the group as well as the development of interactional contracts for personal change.

The Continuing Process of the Group

After individual contracts have been established, and the group begins to manifest sharing and feedback behavior, the role of the leader begins to include the function of processing group transactions. The leader feels free to comment on anything he thinks, feels, sees, or does not understand. The leader will reinforce functional communications, point out dysfunctional processes, and suggest interactional alternatives. The leader attempts to model clear communication, and will ask the group for feedback as to the functionality of the leader's own transactional operations.

Results of the Group

It has been the author's experience that this type of group allows the members to experience (1) a beginning understanding of their own transactional operations; (2) a degree of confidence in the transactional approach; (3) a sense of cohesion with the other group members; (4) more confidence in their own ability to manifest themselves clearly to significant others; and (5) some understanding of what forms of countertransference they may manifest when working with their own clients.

THE SECOND TEN WEEKS: WORKING WITH COUPLES

During the second ten weeks, the participants are provided didactic, experiential, and role play presentations geared toward helping them understand on both a cognitive and experiential level various family and marital processes, as well as the assessment, relationship building, contracting, and intervention operations of the marital or family therapist. The participants are asked to read Satir's book, *Conjoint Family Therapy* (Satir, 1964) and Haley's book, *Changing Families* (Haley, 1971). Satir's book is, in the author's opinion, one of the best basic texts on family therapy presently on the market. Haley's book is an excellent collection of family therapy articles that present a wide variety of orientations by many different leaders in the family therapy field. A third book that is recommended is Glick and Kessler's (1974) book, *Marital and Family Therapy*. In addition, the participants are given a copy of a handout, "Family Therapy: Using a Transactional Orientation," written by this author (Lantz, 1977). The handout is a summary of information presented in Chapters One, Two, and Three of this volume. Andrews' book, *The Emotionally Disturbed Family* (1974) is also recommended.

The Initial Presentation

Initially a didactic presentation that follows the handout is provided for the participants. After this presentation, the participants listen to a recording of a marital therapy session, which is presented in this book as Chapter Five. This tape is used because it illustrates a number of dysfunctional marital processes, a good example of countertransference (this helps the participants feel free to talk about their own countertransference problems), a number of productive therapeutic interventions, and finally, because it illustrates in a fairly dramatic fashion the positive benefits that can result when the marital relationship members change dysfunctional communication patterns.

An Experiential Exercise

After a discussion of the tape, the participants engage in an experiential exercise. The purpose of the exercise is to allow the trainees to experience how it feels to be a member of an avoid-avoid relationship, an attack-avoid relationship, and an attack-attack relationship. The participants break up into dyads and both members of the dyad are instructed to ignore and avoid the other member. After about five minutes, the members are requested to act out a relationship where one member attacks and the other member avoids. The roles are then reversed. Next, the participants are asked to simulate an attack-attack relationship; five minutes are allowed for this experience. After each type of relationship has been experienced, the participants are asked to discuss (1) how they felt, (2) which role was most comfortable for them, and (3) which role was least comfortable. This experience helps the participants recognize the more common dysfunctional marital interactional styles.

Role Playing

After the exercises, the participants engage in marital therapy role-playing simulations. One participant is therapist, one participant is husband, and one participant is wife. The husband and wife are asked to role play a marital conflict situation which, from what they know of themselves and each other, might develop if they were married to one another. Chairs are set up in the middle of the room for the therapy simulation and the rest of the participants are seated around the action. The simulation is recorded on audiovisual equipment. Approximately twenty minutes are allowed for each simulation. The therapist's interventions are critiqued by the training leader and the other group participants for the rest of the hour, by going over the tape. Two simulations and critiques can occur in every two-hour session. Over eight or nine weeks, each participant can be therapist at least two times and can be a marital relationship member at least two times. The amount of time in the therapist role can be increased if the participants want to role play using a co-therapist.

The Critique

During the critique period, the participants who were clients in the role simulation are asked to point out to the therapist which interventions were helpful (i.e., the client began to want to change), and which were not (i.e., the client increased his or her resistance to change). In many instances, the client simulators will break out of the client role and in such instances it is often found that the therapist did something that made it difficult for the simulation clients to continue in their dysfunctional interactional roles.

By reviewing the tape, the group is able to pick out instances where the therapist simulator allowed him or herself to get pulled into the marital pathology. The therapist simulators can often pick up on their own avoidance and how this occurs by becoming overly interested in content as opposed to the marital process. Instances in which the therapist simulator manifested himself in an unclear or incongruent way are also reviewed. Functional and workable interventions are highlighted by the client simulators who can help tell the therapist "what you did that worked and was helpful." During the marital therapy critique the instructor focuses upon helping the participants recognize and deal with coding and decoding distortions. During the final ten weeks, the focus is stretched to include a focus upon family structure.

THE FINAL TEN WEEKS: WORKING WITH FAMILIES

In the final ten weeks, the instructor's goal is to build awareness of family structure issues. Family structure refers to the pattern and flow of family interaction in families that include issues of cross generational overinvolvement. The trainees are asked to simulate families that include at least three people and two generations. At least four different family therapy simulations are set up. The simulations are a therapist working with (1) a father-daughter coalition against the mother; (2) a rigid generational boundary between parents and children that prevents nurturing within the family; (3) a family where the child acts out when the parents manifest conflict; and (4) a family that includes an adult who is overly involved with his or her mother, forcing the spouse to become overly involved with one of the children. Again, all simulations are recorded and the critique process remains essentially the same.

SUMMARY

The author has presented a fomat for beginning training in marital and family therapy. The approach includes both cognitive and experiential learning. The approach takes thirty weeks using two hours per week and can easily be included in most academic or staff development training programs.

10

Co-Therapy in Marital
and Family Therapy

In his recent book, Haley (1976) presents the view that "the use of a
co-therapist is usually for the security of the clinician and not for the
value to the client." He further points out that at present, outcome
studies have not proved that it provides either improved or faster results. Although Haley has raised an important question, it is the author's view that the co-therapy approach does in fact provide family
and therapist with certain opportunities for therapeutic interaction not
available in any other therapy system form. The purpose of this chapter
is to present some of the advantages, disadvantages, and practical considerations in the use of the co-therapist team during the family
therapy or martial therapy process (Lantz, 1978).

DISADVANTAGES IN CO-THERAPY

The major disadvantage in using the co-therapy approach is that it
increases the complexity in the family therapy situation (Andrews,

Sections of this chapter appeared in "Co-therapy Approach in Family Therapy." *Social
Work* 23(2): 156–58, March 1978 and are reprinted with the permission of the National
Association of Social Workers, Inc.

1976). For example, in a marital therapy session involving husband, wife, and therapist, there are six possible transactions (from husband to wife, from wife to husband, from husband to therapist, from therapist to husband, from wife to therapist and from therapist to wife). With the addition of a co-therapist the number of possible transactions increases from six to twelve (from husband to wife, from wife to husband, from husband to therapist 1, from therapist 1 to husband, from husband to therapist 2, from therapist 2 to husband, from wife to therapist 1, from therapist 1 to wife, from wife to therapist 2, from therapist 2 to wife, from therapist 1 to therapist 2, and from therapist 2 to therapist 1). This increase in the number of transactions is illustrated in Figure 14.

In other words, the complexity of the therapy situation is doubled. Such an increase in complexity will make it difficult for the co-therapist team to keep track of transactions and is generally not worth the time and effort unless there are specific advantages to be gained by adding a co-therapist. The additional cost (i.e., the family must pay two therapists in co-therapy) is also not justified unless there are very clear reasons for the use of the co-therapist team. The following illustrations will point out some appropriate uses of co-therapy.

CO-THERAPY TO HELP PROVIDE A CLIMATE OF SUPPORT AND CONFRONTATION

As Andrews (1965, 1974) has noted, therapy approaches geared toward transactional change must include a climate of extensive defense confrontation and emotional support. Without extensive defense confrontation the family members will probably be unable to change. Without extensive emotional support, the family will probably not tolerate the confrontation and may not return for further therapy. Recently this view has been supported by research evidence developed by both Truax and Mitchell (1971) and by Fix and Haffke (1976).

The co-therapy approach in family and marital therapy increases the ability of this therapy subsystem to provide a balanced amount of support and confrontation in a wide variety of ways. The family as a group and each individual member can receive both support and confrontation at the same time through the use of the co-therapy approach. This is often difficult with only one therapist. In addition, with the use of a male and female co-therapist team the family as a whole and each individual member can receive support and confrontation from both a male and female. In certain circumstances such flexibility is necessary (Lantz, 1978).

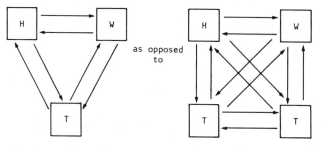

Figure 14. *Increased complexity*

For example, one couple's primary dysfunctional interactional sequence included a somewhat dominating wife's verbal blaming whenever she felt hurt and a passive husband's avoidance whenever the wife brought up any discussion of problems or concerns. The husband's passivity fed the wife's blaming which in turn fed the husband's passivity. The couple were being seen by a female therapist who was in the position of (1) reinforcing the couple's process whenever she confronted the husband and (2) helping the wife feel more left out and alone whenever she supported the husband. In addition, the husband would point out how he was "right" whenever the female therapist confronted the wife. Any attempts by the therapist to support the wife were viewed by the husband as "two females who don't understand." The situation was dramatically changed with the addition of a male co-therapist. The husband was able to tolerate confrontation from the male co-therapist and such confrontation did not model the couple's own dysfunctional process. The addition of the co-therapist enabled each therapist to rely on the other for the supportive maneuver whenever it was needed. This allowed the continuation of extensive defense confrontation within the conjoint sessions. The couple remained in therapy and was able to change.

THE USE OF CO-THERAPY FOR MODELING

Modeling approaches for inducing behavioral and interactional change may well have amassed more research data indicating their effectiveness than any other therapy approach (e.g., see Bandura, 1971 and Fix and Haffke, 1976). The use of a male and female co-therapist team provides the total family group an excellent opportunity for learning through imitation, modeling, and identification, as illustrated in the following example (Lantz, 1978).

Mr. and Mrs. Ray requested marital therapy complaining of an unhappy marital situation in which they both felt they no longer "know each other very well." The couple stated that they seldom spent time together and that sexual relations were becoming more and more infrequent. The couple's primary dysfunctional transactional sequence included a husband who intellectualized whenever he felt anxiety or emotional pain and a wife who used avoidance to control what she considered unacceptable angry feelings. The husband's intellectualization defense, used whenever he felt emotional pain, was viewed by the wife as "talking down to me." The wife's avoidance was viewed by the husband as evidence that "she doesn't care." The couple was seen by a male and female co-therapy team. The team modeled for the couple how to manifest feelings and how to resolve conflict. Both members of the co-therapy team commented openly and directly to each other whenever they felt angry, nervous, hurt or wanted the other co-therapist to change behavior. Both husband and wife were able to imitate this approach. Over a seven-month period the couple became more comfortable expressing feelings. The husband gave up his use of intellectualization and the wife was able to become angry without her usual fear. When asked what had been most helpful during the conjoint sessions both Mr. and Mrs. Ray agreed that the co-therapists comfort in dealing directly with each other had been "a great help."

CO-THERAPY AS ON THE SPOT SUPERVISION

As Curry (1966) has noted, the forming together of the family and the therapist results in a "family therapy system." According to Curry this new system operates as does any other system in that all subsystems will feel the pull of the larger system's influence. As a result, the therapist subsystem will often find itself acting in accordance with the other systems' dysfunctional communication rules. Even experienced clinicians can not always avoid this systems influence. Co-therapists can minimize the antitherapeutic elements in this phenomenon by actively supervising each other during the family therapy sessions.

For example, in a recent marital therapy session with a couple which used an attack-attack interactional style to maintain semicontact without the risk of intimacy, the author's co-therapist pointed out that he was talking to the couple in a voice that was as loud and high pitched as the couple's interactions. After this comment, the author became aware of the irritation he was feeling towards the couple. In this instance, the author had joined with the couple in their interactional game. The co-therapist's comment helped the author become aware of his colusion and he was able to lower his voice in a way that modeled a more constructive interactional approach.

CO-THERAPY AND THE USE OF A ONE-WAY MIRROR

In recent years family therapists have been using interviewing rooms with one way mirrors in a variety of ways (e.g., see Minuchin, 1974). The use of a co-therapist in family therapy can help family members gain insight into alternative forms of interaction through the process of watching with one therapist as the other co-therapist relates to other family members from behind a one-way mirror.

For example, Mrs. Riley requested services complaining that her seven-year-old son was "bad." The problems apparently started after Mrs. Riley's husband died in a car crash. Prior to the car accident, Mr. Riley had taken care of most family discipline problems. Mrs. Riley's interactions with her son largely consisted of frequent nagging and very little consistent limiting behavior. Part of the family therapy process was geared toward helping Mrs. Riley learn some new child management skills. Mrs. Riley and the male co-therapist spent part of some family sessions behind a one-way mirror watching the female co-therapist relate to the son. It was explained to Mrs. Riley that in view of her son's "special problems" we wanted her to watch the female co-therapist demonstrate some "special" techniques that Mrs. Riley needed to use at home in order to help her son. The female co-therapist actively rewarded the son for positive behavior and limited the son's inappropriate behavior in a pleasant but firm manner. The male co-therapist explained exactly what the female co-therapist was doing and pointed out the positive results. Mrs. Riley was able to learn the approach. The use of co-therapists allowed Mrs. Riley the opportunity to receive an explanation of the procedure while it was being modeled by the female co-therapist.

CO-THERAPY TO INCREASE OPPORTUNITIES FOR THERAPEUTIC COALITIONS

Both Haley (1976) and Minuchin (1974) have described the use of deliberate coalitions between the therapist and a family subsystem to facilitate family structural change. A therapist can facilitate reaching out behavior on the part of a distant spouse by flirting with the spouse

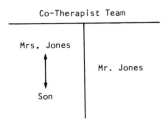

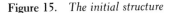

Figure 15. *The initial structure*

of opposite gender to the therapist (Haley, 1976). The therapist can help de-scapegoat the identified patient in a family by mimicking the behavior of the scapegoated individual. This approach changes the family situation through the therapist's coalition with the identified patient by relabeling the identified patient's behavior as normal (Minuchin, 1974). The use of a male and female co-therapy team greatly increases the options for therapeutic coalitions (Lantz, 1978).

For example, in the Jones family, Mrs. Jones was overinvolved with her eleven-year-old son. Mr. Jones was isolated from the mother-son dyad. The family's structure, illustrated in Figure 15, resulted in the son's refusal to go to school or to speak with any adults other than his mother.

Family treatment was geared toward developing a dyad between father and mother and toward decreasing interaction between mother and son. In this case, the co-therapists decided to use activities as a context for treatment, partially due to the son's refusal to use verbal forms of interaction. The son took an immediate dislike to the male co-therapist. This dislike was used as leverage for change when the male co-therapist challenged the son to a game of checkers. The female co-therapist suggested that the father be on the son's side by

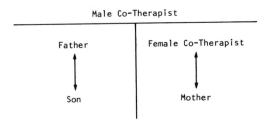

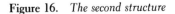

Figure 16. *The second structure*

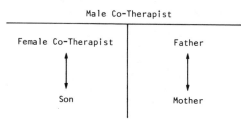

Figure 17. *Mother and father as dyad*

cheering for the son "against" the male co-therapist while the female co-therapist watched with the mother. The family structure was then briefly changed as is illustrated in Figure 16. During this structure the son and father were able to verbally interact.

After a number of weeks and a variety of "checker-playing configuration steps," the female co-therapist suggested that she and the son challenge mother and father. During this structure, as illustrated in Figure 17, the son was able to verbalize with the female co-therapist. The male co-therapist loudly rooted for the parents against the son-female co-therapist dyad.

This game marked the beginning of work on strengthening the marital dyad. From this point on, the female co-therapist remained somewhat in coalition with the son as the male co-therapist worked with the marital pair. It is important to note that the multiple structural combinations and elements needed in the handling of this case would have been impossible to develop without a male and female co-therapy team.

SUMMARY

Although co-therapy increases the therapy system complexity and is a costly procedure, there are times when it is necessary and/or advisable. The author has presented five case illustrations demonstrating specific rationales for the co-therapy approach. It is hoped that this discussion will be found useful to other family therapists as they are thinking through their own use of the co-therapy approach.

11

Family-Centered Therapy and the Vicious Circle

Since the late 1950s, the variety of therapy forms aimed at changing the functioning of the family group has grown at a tremendous rate of speed. When reviewing the family therapy literature, it is interesting to note that many different therapy approaches have been documented as having positive influence upon the functioning of the total family group. This may indicate that there are certain common variables consistently used by therapists from a wide variety of orientations, that if identified could provide a general framework that would give us more rigorous practical family therapy guidelines concerning what to do and who to include. Articles (Hoffman, 1976, and Wender, 1968) describing what is often called in everyday language "the vicious circle" may point the way toward identifying such a general framework. It is the purpose of this chapter to expand upon the vicious circle concept by presenting a family functioning map of the territory in which vicious circles often occur and to provide for the reader a set of assessment and intervention guidelines that can be used in family-centered therapy approaches aimed at breaking up dysfunctional vicious circles.

THE VICIOUS CIRCLE

Hoffman (1976) has described one form of the vicious circle which she calls the homeostatic cycle. In her article the concept is illustrated by example rather than rigorously defined. Her examples show a set of patterned sequence behaviors between people that tend to be repeated over time. It is hypothesized that such cycles may serve the function of avoiding or preventing other family behaviors as has been suggested by Bateson (1967). Another theory is that such patterns may simply snowball due to the role of deviation amplifying feedback, as has been suggested by both Marujama (1963) and Wender (1968).

Although Hoffman illustrates the homeostatic variety of the vicious circle primarily by using triadic examples including two parents and a child, it has been this author's experience that many forms of the vicious circle can occur in an individual and dyad or triad context.

INDIVIDUAL, DYAD, AND TRIAD VICIOUS CIRCLES

A good example of the individual form of the vicious circle may occur with an athlete who is beginning to lose some of his or her speed and coordination. The sequence goes as follows:

1. The athlete's physical abilities begin to decrease with age.
2. The athlete evaluates the decrease in ability as a serious threat to identity.
3. The athlete avoids competition to insulate against the pain of the evaluation.
4. Avoiding competition amplifies the decrease in performance.
5. The athlete experiences a greater threat to identity.
6. There is an increased avoidance of competition, etc.

A common example of the dyadic vicious circle may occur between an aggressive wife and a passive husband, which can be illustrated by the following sequence of events.

1. The husband experiences anxiety associated with contact with his wife.
2. The husband avoids anxiety by withdrawing from the wife.
3. The wife feels left out and alone.
4. The wife yells at her husband in an attempt to make contact.
5. The husband increases avoidance behavior. .

6. The wife feels even more alone and increases her yelling attempts to make contact, etc.

A common form of a triadic cycle operates as follows.

1. A teen-age son yells at his mother.
2. The mother complains to her husband rather than talking to the son.
3. The husband scolds the son in a half-hearted way.
4. The son yells at his mother again.
5. The mother complains to her husband.
6. The husband tells his wife that she can't handle kids.
7. The son continues to yell at his mother.
8. The wife complains to her husband.
9. The husband becomes positive that his wife is the problem, etc.

TWO MAJOR CLASSES OF THE VICIOUS CIRCLE

There are two major classes of the vicious circle and each class can occur in an individual and dyad or triad situation. Both forms can also be in operation at the same time in the same situation and often tend to feed each other. The first class is the type that can be called the "snowball" or deviation amplifying form of the vicious circle. This form was, to my knowledge, originally identified by Marujama (1963) and has been further elaborated upon in the context of psychotherapy by Wender (1968). This form of vicious circle is similar to a snowball rolling down a hill. As the snowball moves it picks up weight, which then causes it to move faster. It then picks up even more weight, moves faster, picks up more weight, moves faster and so on and so on. The previously used example of the athlete is a form of this snowball vicious circle. In that example, the athlete's decreased performance was evaluated as a threat to identify and led to an avoidance of competition, which amplified the deviation in performance. This then amplified the negative evaluation and the threat to identity. The net effect is a circular process that escalates over time. It has been this author's experience that deviation amplifying circles are easier to interpret than the homeostatic circles described by Hoffman in both individual and dyad and triad situations.

A second form of vicious circle has been labeled by Hoffman (1976) as the homeostatic cycle. The homeostatic cycle functions in a way that creates a symptom that will prevent other behaviors. This process often is noted at child guidance and mental health centers that work with children and their parents. A common example of this vicious circle in a triadic form can be called the minor as marital therapist syndrome. In this process, the parents have covertly agreed not to discuss with each other any problems, issues, conflicts, or concerns in their marriage. As a result, both parents experience unresolved anger which is then usually denied. From time to time, the anger surfaces and at this point one of the children will get anxious and will develop some sort of symptom. The parental conflict is immediately dropped as the parents work together to help the child. The child is reinforced for its symptom development and the parents are reinforced by the relief they feel about not having to deal with their conflicts. The child's symptom functions to prevent parental conflict and acts as a cement for the parents' marriage. The process is circular and usually continues at least until the child has developed a set of behaviors that can be given a psychiatric label. Even after such labeling has occurred, the process may well continue unless the professional helper can involve the parents in a process of working out some of their marital problems. It has been this author's experience that the homeostatic circle is more difficult to interrupt than the deviation amplifying circle.

VICIOUS CIRCLES CAN OCCUR AT DIFFERENT RATES OF SPEED

Not only can the two major classes of the vicious circle occur in both individual and dyad and triad forms, but they can also occur at different rates of speed. The previously mentioned minor as marital therapist sequence can usually be identified in its entirety as occurring during a family therapy session lasting from one to one and one-half hours in length. On the other hand, some vicious circles will not be completed in less than one year's time. For example, an associate recently presented a case where the identified patient was regularly hospitalized for at least three weeks around the same time every year. Once a year the client would develop a profound psychotic depression just prior to the redetermination hearing about his psychiatric disability. Disability payments were in this way guaranteed for at least another year. Any complete assessment of this vicious circle sequence could not be made without a good history, as the process would not be manifested in its entirety during a single therapy session. The fact that vicious circles occur at different speed rates is important to remember, as in many instances those family therapists who do not believe in the use of history or any other data that is not completely experiential in nature may well miss many important clues that could identify a vicious circle sequence.

VICIOUS CIRCLES CAN OCCUR BETWEEN DIFFERENT CATEGORIES OF PEOPLE

In most instances, the vicious circle will occur in a dyad or triad form and will develop between individuals from the same family group. However, at times the vicious circle will include one or more individuals who are outside of the family group's boundary but within the identified patient's boundary of socially and emotionally significant people. In certain instances, the vicious circle will be individual in nature and will not involve significant others. However, in practice this is fairly rare. Sometimes the vicious circle will occur between the family as a group and various social agencies and organizations. It is important to remember that vicious circles can occur between different categories of people and institutions; if this is not remembered, the family-centered therapist may develop rigid rules about the composition of family therapy sessions. Such rules often exclude important segments of the vicious circle sequence or on the other hand, such rules may result in the therapist including individuals who are not relevant to the problem at hand. As a general rule, it is valuable to look to the members of the natural family group as the most likely people to be involved with the identified patient in a vicious circle. If the complete sequence cannot be identified after examining the natural family group, it is important to screen other individuals within the identified patient's social and emotional network. If a thorough search of the individuals within the family and social boundaries of the identified patient does not reveal the participants in the vicious circle, it may then be safe to assume that the vicious circle is individual in nature. The following social functioning map is presented to help the clinician identify the areas of territory in which vicious circles may occur (Fig. 18).

ASSESSMENT GUIDELINES

It is important for the family-centered therapist to remember that when an individual manifests emotional pain or develops any behavior that has traditionally been called a psychiatric symptom, that individual may be signaling the presence of a vicious circle sequence. After re-

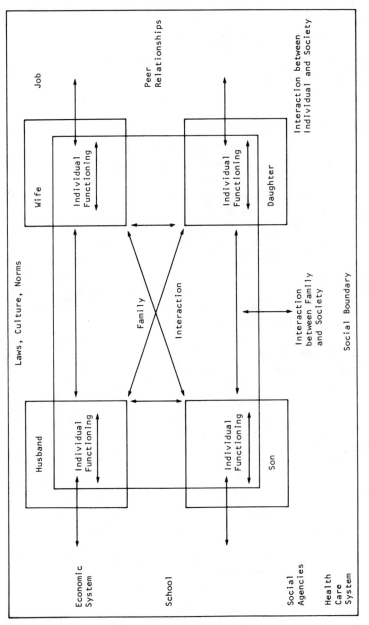

Figure 18. *Social functioning territory map*

ceiving such a signal, the family-centered therapist begins an assessment process that should result in the identification of the following:

1. The type of vicious circle in which the identified patient is involved (is it a deviation amplifying process, a homeostatic cycle process, or some combination of the two?).
2. The identification of who is participating in the vicious circle sequence (is the circle an individual or dyad or triad process?).
3. The identification of the speed of the vicious circle sequence (is it slow or fast, acute or chronic?).
4. The identification of the social functioning territory in which the vicious circle occurs (does it cross individual, family, or social boundaries, and what categories of people and institutions are involved?).
5. And most importantly, what blocking procedures can the family-centered therapist use that will most effectively and efficiently interrupt the vicious circle sequence allowing more functional patterns to emerge?

INTERVENTION GUIDELINES

Intervention procedures depend upon the type, form, and speed of the vicious circle as well as the territory in which it occurs. If the vicious circle is of the deviation amplifying form, intervention approaches can be fairly direct. For example, in the illustration where the wife yelled at the husband, who avoided contact, which caused the wife to escalate the yelling, a simple directive, such as having the wife avoid the husband, may well interrupt and change the entire process. On the other hand, where the vicious circle is of the homeostatic form, the therapist may need to use a series of interventions which will bring the avoided behavior out into the open. For example, one way of interrupting the minor as marital therapist syndrome is for the therapist to relabel the efforts of the marital pair to help the child as "evidence illustrating differences and conflict between the husband and wife." Such relabeling places the child in the position where the child's symptom no longer prevents marital conflict and as a result, the symptom will often disappear. The direction of therapy can then be changed to help the marital pair work through some of their problems.

Vicious circles that include two, three, or more participating individuals can usually be handled most effectively in conjoint interviews. The conjoint interview allows the vicious circle process to occur experientially in front of the therapist and as a result more data and opportunities for intervention are manifested. Vicious circles that involve only one person's participation can also be treated in a conjoint interview by relabeling the vicious circle process as a way the individual obtains or avoids contact with others. This changes the vicious circle into a transactional process and increases opportunities for change. Group treatment is often used when the client does not have a significant other whom the therapist and client can involve in the helping process.

When the vicious circle crosses the family boundary to include individuals who are not a part of the family but who are within the boundary of the identified patient's socially significant people, and who also may act as representatives of various social organizations, the family-centered therapist may have to label their participation as "help for the family or identified patient" rather than as being necessary due to their participation in the vicious circle sequence. Social organization representatives are often quite resistant to seeing the part they may be playing in the vicious circle process. In such instances it may be best to go along with the labeling process of the identified patient and then use the label as a reason for those participants in the vicious circle process who are outside of the family boundary to change some of their actions and behaviors. This does not seem ethical to this author unless the family-centered therapist is willing to view his or her behavior as possibly being a part of the vicious circle process. A willingness to include oneself in the diagnosis of the family by the therapist will result in the use of peers and supervisors as an outside monitor to insure that the family-centered therapist's efforts to help do not become a part of the problem.

When the vicious circle sequence goes at a slow rate of speed, the therapist's first intervention goal may need to be speeding up of the process. The faster the speed of the vicious circle sequence, the more likely it is that change can occur. The speed can be increased by adding individuals to the therapy sessions, by prescribing the signal symptom and asking that the identified patient escalate his or her production of symptomatic behavior, or by creating a crisis. For example, in the illustration where the client developed a psychotic depression once a year just prior to his redetermination hearing, the process could be speeded up by getting the redetermination hearing rescheduled every three months instead of once a year.* This would

---

*(Author's Note: the ethics of such a move would require a great deal of discussion which cannot occur in a chapter of this length).

increase the rate of the vicious circle sequence, add additional people to the therapy process, and would increase the production of signal symptoms. When the rate is increased, there is also an increase in assessment data, and most importantly, there is a decrease in the stability of the vicious circle sequence.

SUMMARY

Many different forms of therapy seem to have positive influence upon the functioning of the total family group. This may indicate that therapists from a wide variety of orientations often use similar methods that influence family functioning. The author has presented the vicious circle concept as one way of explaining how different therapy approaches can work using similar mechanisms for change. The vicious circle concept was broken down into different elements, such as composition, type, form, speed, and territory, and a set of intervention and assessment guidelines were presented.

12

Family Therapy in Special Situations

From time to time, the family therapist will receive a service request from a family group that presents some form of special circumstance that may require additional knowledge of some form of innovative intervention approach on the part of the family therapist. The purpose of this chapter is to provide a few illustrations of such special circumstances as well as a general discussion of what the family therapist might take into account in each of these cases. Topics to be discussed are (1) families that include a blind family member, (2) families that include a member who has a long history of many psychiatric hospitalizations, (3) child abuse, (4) the family in crisis, (5) the single parent family, and (6) sculpting the family therapy situation (the situation of family and therapist).

THE FAMILY THAT INCLUDES A BLIND FAMILY MEMBER

This author has done family therapy with families that include a blind child, with families that include one or two blind parents, and with a few families in which all family members were blind. The occurrence of blindness in a family group can create special family interactional problems. First, the occurrence of blindness in a family group increases the stress factor for the total family group. The blindness provides the family group with an extra set of family tasks not encountered by most family groups. The family group with a blind family member must negotiate with larger community systems to find and obtain services such as specialized health care, special educational opportunities, as well as many other necessary services. In many communities such services are limited if they exist at all.

Second, the occurrence of blindness in the family group means that the blind family member needs to learn how to decode messages from significant others in a way that is somewhat different from sighted individuals. The blind individual cannot use sight to help him or her decode messages received. Sound, touch, and smell are the receptor senses most available to the blind person, and in many instances individuals who are a part of the blind person's social situation are used to sending nonverbal messages along with verbal output as message qualifiers. Such nonverbal messages are picked up on by other individuals through the sense of sight. Such double coding operations are especially confusing to the blind person.

Blindness can also create problems in terms of family structure. When the family includes two blind parents and a sighted child, the child may use the parents' blindness as a tool for avoiding responsible behavior or as a tool to be used for the purposes of manipulation. This process is illustrated in Figure 19, which shows an overly rigid boundary caused by a block in information flow, due to the blindness, between the blind parents and the sighted child, and the child gaining a position of control over the blind parents.

The goal of family therapy in this type of situation would be to provide resources to the blind parents that could help them develop more effective ways to monitor and correct the child. The use of a homemaker who can see for the parents will often make the communication boundary between the parents and child more permeable. This can then result in the parents regaining a position in which they are more in control and can provide direction to the rest of the family group. The danger in such an approach is that the homemaker might begin to function in the role of parent rather than functioning as a provider of information to the natural parents.

$$\frac{\text{Sighted Child}}{\text{Blind Parents}} \quad \text{as opposed to} \quad \frac{\text{Blind Parents}}{\text{Sighted Child}}$$

Figure 19. *Blind parents and sighted child*

Also, when parents are blind and the child is sighted, the parents will sometimes overly use the child as a sighted guide. In such situations, the child may again develop too much control over the functioning of the family group. Another problem that often occurs is that when the sighted child reaches adolescence and wants to begin spending more time with peers, an overly intense struggle for autonomy may develop between the parents and the adolescent. The parents may become overly dependent upon the adolescent, and as a result, they may hold on too tight when the adolescent begins the natural, age-appropriate process of distancing from the family group. On the other hand, the adolescent may develop intense guilt feelings about leaving his or her parents alone. Again, in such a situation, the family therapy goal is to help the parents gain more control by using resources other than the sighted child. When this occurs, the parents will feel less fear about losing the child.

When the parents are sighted and the child is blind, the parents may at times inhibit the child's progress by being overly concerned about the child. In this situation, the parents are in a position where they must walk a tightrope. The parents must help the child learn certain tasks that other children do not need to learn and this often requires a good bit of extra interaction, direction, guidance, and involvement. On the other hand, the parents must not do too much for the child or the child may begin to use his or her blindness as a tool for parental manipulation. A common dysfunctional family structure often found when the child is blind can be illustrated as in Figure 20. This structure does not include a boundary between generations.

The following case presentation is provided to illustrate a few methods that the family therapist can use when working with a family that includes a blind family member.

The Carpenter Family

The Carpenter family, consisting of Jack (the 45-year-old father), Mary (the 45-year-old mother), and Barb (the 16-year-old daughter), requested family therapy in the early part of 1976. The father had been

Figure 20.   *Sighted parents and blind child*

blind since birth and the mother, who had a sight problem since birth, became completely blind at around the age of 11. The parents met each other while attending a school for the blind and, at the time of family therapy, had been married over 20 years. Mrs. Carpenter is self-employed. She runs a small business in a state office building where she prepares and sells sandwiches and drinks for individuals who work in the office building. Mr. Carpenter is a switchboard operator at a small factory. Barb was a sophomore in high school and at the time of treatment was spending a good bit of her time driving her parents to and from work and was in charge of many of the family household chores.

The parents requested family therapy explaining that Barb had become "belligerent" and "sassy" in the last few months. The parents were concerned that the daughter might be hanging around with undesirable classmates. The daughter wanted to spend more and more time away from home. The parents stated that Barb was willing to come for family therapy and an initial family interview was scheduled.

In the initial family interview, the family therapist was greeted by a very pleasant 16-year-old adolescent who introduced the therapist to her parents, walked her parents over to two empty chairs in the office and asked the therapist "where should we start?" During the interview the parents complained about the daughter's "back talk" and "disrespectful attitude." The parents insisted that the daughter was being disrespectful and sassy during the interview, although the family therapist experienced the daughter's behavior and actions during the interview as quite respectful and appropriate. The therapist was becoming very confused until he remembered that his experience of the daughter was, in fact, different from the parents' experience, as he was able to see the daughter and the parents were not able to see her. The therapist decided to close his eyes during the interview so that he could gain a better perspective of the parents' experience. Interestingly, when the therapist could not see the daughter, her voice did in fact sound belligerant and sassy. In this instance the daughter's nonverbal messages (i.e., smile, physical posture, etc.) served as message qualifiers that could not be picked up on by the blind parents. Intervention in this situation consisted of having the daughter touch the parents and give nonverbal messages through her hands as she was telling her parents about her concerns, resentments, and problems. This approach worked and the family members were able to resolve many of their conflicts. The use of the daughter's hands as the tool for sending nonverbal messages allowed the parents to feel that the daughter did care even as she was verbalizing her resentments, concerns, and desire for time away from home.

WORKING WITH FAMILIES THAT INCLUDE A MEMBER WHO HAS A LONG HISTORY OF MANY PSYCHIATRIC HOSPITALIZATIONS

With the advent of the community mental health movement, many family therapists working in a community mental health setting are now working with clients and client families that have experienced many psychiatric hospitalizations and hospitalizations that have lasted for long periods of time. This client population, long ignored and traditionally placed in the back wards of state mental hospitals, is now being recognized as a population group that can be worked with successfully and can be maintained in the community. This new attitude is presently reflected by the National Institute of Mental Health, which has placed programs for aftercare populations as a priority funding item.

The aftercare population can be characterized as having a wide range of problems and concerns which include the following:

1. The aftercare client has generally experienced more than one psychiatric hospitalization, and is generally released from the psychiatric hospital on medication. The client is often not motivated to continue such medication or to seek out services.
2. A large percentage of aftercare clients do not see traditional forms of psychotherapy as relevant to their problems.
3. Aftercare clients are often underskilled and undereducated. Many have not finished high school and have not received any specific vocational training.
4. The aftercare client often has difficulty finding and negotiating the various social service systems in the community.
5. The aftercare client may feel more comfortable in an institutional setting and may resist any approach that has as its goal keeping the client out of the hospital.
6. The aftercare client often is a member of what has been labeled the "multiproblem family." Such families are not always able to provide a stable support base for the individual released from a psychiatric hospital.

7. The aftercare client has often been in the hospital for a long period of time. If this is the case, the client may have lost contact with his or her family and as a result, may not have any significant support group within the community at large.
8. The aftercare client generally requires a period of intense support and intervention using a variety of treatment approaches and involving a number of different support systems in the community if he is to break the cycle of rehospitalization (Knisley and Bussell, 1977).

From a family-centered point of view, it can be generalized that the aftercare client is in or is a part of two different kinds of family situations. The first kind of family situation often encountered by the family therapist who works with the aftercare client can be called the lost family situation. In this situation, the aftercare client has generally been in the hospital for a long period of time and has lost touch with his family of origin and/or family of procreation. The aftercare client's family group may have split up and the various family members may have moved out of the city or state. Sometimes the aftercare client's family may have adjusted to the aftercare client's absence and may wish the situation to remain the same. In such instances, the family may successfully resist the aftercare client's efforts to regain contact. This situation is illustrated in Figure 21, which shows a rigid boundary between the aftercare client and his or her natural family group.

In such a situation, the family therapist will first try to help the aftercare client recontact his or her natural family group. If this is impossible either because of logistics (the family may no longer live in the area) or because of the family's resistance, the family therapist will help the aftercare client build and develop a substitute family group.

Building a substitute family group is a three stage process. The process includes the professional stage, the mixed stage, and the natural stage. In the professional stage the family therapist attempts to get the aftercare client in contact with as many professional helpers and professional support systems as possible. The client could be re-

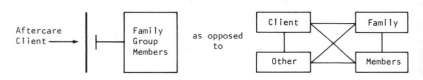

Figure 21. *The lost family situation*

ferred to a day treatment program, a psychiatrist for medication, a group therapy program, a public health nurse, a vocational rehabilitation counselor, a caseworker at a public assistance agency, a housing specialist, an employment agency, a medical clinic, a settlement house, and as many other agencies or professionals as can be reasonably coordinated. The goals in this stage include (1) helping the aftercare client obtain supportive services; (2) helping the aftercare client stay busy and occupied as much as possible; (3) helping the client learn to negotiate and make contact with as many different systems and people as possible; and (4) teaching the aftercare client a set of skills (i.e., how to meet people, how to ride the bus, how to fill out job applications, how to dress for a job interview, how to find an apartment, how to get on public assistance, how to find a doctor, etc.), which the client will find personally helpful and can then teach to other aftercare clients.

In the mixed stage of the substitute family rebuilding process, the client joins an aftercare client group. The group is a problem-solving group made up of other aftercare clients and at least two professionals. The purpose of the group is to help the group members identify common problems, give each other support, and help the group members share with each other any problem solutions, skills, and resources that the group members may have at their disposal. The group leaders attempt to keep the members involved with each other and to help the group members offer each other support in a specific way. For example, in a recent group meeting, one member who had just been released from a state hospital stated that he would like to go bowling, but that he was afraid. Another group member offered to take him and followed through by doing so. The following week, the recently released client reported that he had signed up for a bowling league and that he was not quite so sure he wanted to return to the hospital.

During the mixed stage, the aftercare clients begin to give, take, and receive support from other aftercare clients, as well as from the various professional helpers. In the group setting, the aftercare client begins to develop relationships with individuals who share common experiences and have many common concerns. Friendships are made and invariably relationship difficulties occur. When this happens, the client and the client's recently developed significant other are offered relationship therapy in conjoint interviews. At this point, the client has moved from the mixed to the natural stage of the substitute family group building process.

In the natural stage the aftercare client and the client's significant other are involved in conjoint interviews that focus upon the relationship pair's interactional process. In this stage, the focus is changed from problem-solving about common environmental or adjustment concerns to include problem-solving focused upon the relationship members' transactional process. At this point, both the aftercare client and his or her newly developed significant other have started to develop a relationship, make significant emotional contact with another human being, and are involved in the common human concern of learning to be with another in a functional and healthy way. The client's isolation is challenged, the client begins to make a commitment to living as opposed to avoiding life by withdrawing into a hospital setting, and the client is provided the opportunity to learn to solve and deal with relationship problems as opposed to avoiding them by focusing upon, exacerbating, or developing a chronic mental condition.

The second type of family situation often encountered by the family therapist working with the aftercare client can be called the unstructured family situation. In this type of family situation the family group generally has failed to develop effective boundaries between family members and also has failed to develop an effective generational boundary between parents and the children (Bowen, 1960). This family situation can be illustrated as in Figure 22.

In the unstructured family situation, the various family members have great difficulty differentiating their own self from the other family members. Coding, decoding, and family structural processes are all three distorted and confused. There is confusion about family roles and the family members are provided little opportunity to meet their needs for sense-order and production. The family therapist's goal when working with the unstructured family situation is to introduce as much clarity, order, and role definition as possible into the dysfunctional family system. This can be done in a variety of different ways which include (1) task assignment, (2) reinforcing differentness, and (3) scheduling.

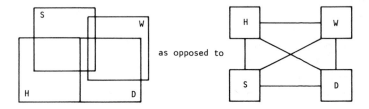

Figure 22. *The unstructured family situation*

When using task assignment the family therapist attempts to get the unstructured family group members to define specific goals that they wish to accomplish. After the various family members are helped to define specific goals, the therapist gives each family member a different task assignment to be accomplished which will help the family group achieve its defined goal. Introducing different tasks for different family members helps the family therapist show the various family members that they have different skills, different opinions, and different interests. Differentness is reinforced as a positive quality, and the operationalizing of such differentness through the various task assignments helps the family members reinforce and/or develop boundaries between the self and other. Scheduling further reinforces the concept of differentness and boundaries by providing different tasks to be accomplished by different family members during different periods of time. Again, family boundaries are reinforced.

In addition to the task assignments, reinforcement of differentness, and the scheduling procedures, the family therapist also attempts to get each family group member involved with a variety of different helping professionals and social service agencies. This can increase support for the family group and also help in the differentiation process. When mother goes to the welfare department to apply for assistance and father goes to the job counselor and the son goes to an activity group at a settlement house, the family system is again involved in a process that reinforces the concepts of individual differentness, separation, and individual boundaries. In general, it can be assumed that with an increase in the development of boundaries within the family group, there will be a decrease in the aftercare client's production of severe emotional signal symptoms.

CHILD ABUSE

Only recently has child abuse been viewed as a family affair. Traditionally, treatment has been based on the concept of the child as a victim of parental pathology and services have been directed toward placement of the child in a more favorable environment, as well as punishment for the abusing parent or parents. In recent years, this approach has been modified to include an attempt to understand how the child and/or spouse of the abusing parents plays into the process, and also an attempt to avoid placement of the child in an institution or foster home if possible, and to work with the family as a total group.

This newer approach recognizes the family as a natural group that can modify dysfunctional transactions which often result in the act of child abuse (Helfer and Kempe, 1972).

The act of child abuse seems to be largely associated with the following factors:

1. The parent who abuses a child was often also abused as a child.
2. The parent who abuses a child often feels isolated and sees very little opportunity to receive help, although such help may be available.
3. At times the parent who abuses a child will see the child as being somewhat different from the parents' other children.
4. The parent who abuses a child will often report unresolved marital conflict between the abusing parent and his or her spouse.
5. The abused child and the spouse of the abusing parent will often protect the abusing parent from the authorities and will often deny that such a problem exists.
6. The abusing parent may have unrealistic ideas about what one should expect from children.
7. Some form of crisis often exists that will set in motion the family transactions which may result in child abuse (Helfer and Kempe, 1972; Holmes et al., 1973).

It has been this author's experience that child abuse is best viewed as a rather dangerous signal symptom of dysfunction in the total family group. As a result, treatment should include both protection for the battered or abused child and help for the family as a total group. With this in mind, the following treatment concepts and generalizations can be used to help the abusing family.

First, the helping professional will seldom be given a very clear message from family members that child abuse is occurring within the family group. Often a family member will drop a clue rather than provide an open admission that there is a child abuse problem. If the professional picks up on the clue and asks various family members about the possibility of child abuse, the family members will often deny that abuse is occurring. Even the victim may find it difficult to report the problem. The following list of frequently dropped clues was developed by Holmes et al. (1973) and provides guidelines for the professional practitioner that can often predict the occurrence of child abuse. When several of these clues are manifested in the same family, there is a good chance that child abuse may be occurring. The child abuse indicators include the following:

1. The parent often will express a fear of being abusive to his or her child.
2. The parent will often express a fear of losing control of his or her emotions.
3. The family has often been referred for treatment by a referral source that suspects the occurrence of abuse within the family group.
4. The parent does not wish to focus upon or talk about a child's injury.
5. A child develops a pattern of running away from home.
6. The parent will give a child punishment that is clearly out of proportion to the child's behavior, which may suggest that the punishment serves a displacement function for the parent's anger.
7. The parent manifests unrealistic expectations for the child that often include nurturing of the parent by the child.
8. The parent views the child's behavior as deliberate abuse of the parent by the child.
9. The parent requests placement of the child.
10. The family home is either very sloppy or very immaculate.
11. The child is blamed for marital conflict.
12. The child does not cry when spanked.
13. The parent feels that his own parents' inappropriate child raising techniques were justified.
14. The parent is unable to show the child affection.
15. The child frequently suffers from unexplained or poorly explained injuries that often require medical attention.
16. The parent often calls the child such names as "devil," "bastard," or "whore."
17. The parent may report that a relative or friend abuses their children.

It has been this author's experience that the family therapist who suspects that a family/client is, in fact, engaged in a child abuse process, should be open with the family members about this concern. In many instances, the family therapist should tell the family that the therapist has a need and ethical responsibility to report his or her concerns to the proper authorities. If this is done in a concerned and nonjudgemental way, the family will often feel a great sense of relief and will then openly admit the problem. The following conversation is reported from the author's memory (i.e., the interview was not tape recorded) and illustrates what often occurs when the family therapist states his or her concerns and ethical responsibilities to the family in a nonjudgemental and supportive way.

THERAPIST:

[To parents] I am concerned about what I see here today. Johnny has a black eye and you both have been drinking. How did he get the black eye?

HUSBAND:

[Looking away] He fell down.

THERAPIST:

[To parents] You have been drinking. When you drink, you often lose your temper. Did either of you lose your temper and strike Johnny?

HUSBAND:

He fell down.

THERAPIST:

I have trouble believing this. I need to tell you that I am going to report what I see and my concerns to the child welfare agency. I believe you have been hitting Johnny. I don't think you want to do this but that you are afraid to bring up the problem.

[Wife begins to cry.]

[Husband is silent and is looking away.]

THERAPIST:

Is it clear what I am going to do?

WIFE:

[Crying] Yes.

HUSBAND:

I don't want to hurt him but I lose my temper [crying].

THERAPIST:

[Softly] Okay. It's good it's out in the open. Now we can work on it.

In many instances, after such a confrontation, the family will get very angry at the therapist. They may tell the therapist that they are going to bring legal action against the therapist, they may at times threaten the therapist with physical violence, but in almost every instance that this author has experienced, the family has not followed through on such threats and has returned for further treatment.

When the family therapist has decided that child abuse is in fact a problem, the treatment focus is directed at protecting the child and helping the parents develop the necessary controls that can prevent such abuse in the future. It is often necessary and helpful to report the incident of child abuse to the proper authorities. In some states, such as Ohio, this is required by law. Frequently, the child welfare agency will accept the report, but will not see it as necessary to become involved on a protective service basis if the family is willing to continue in treatment. In some instances, it is beneficial for the child welfare agency to open a case on the family and gain temporary protective custody of the child. At times temporary placement of the child in a foster home or group home is in fact necessary to protect the child.

In most instances, the family will find the reporting of the abuse incident as helpful. If the family knows that the appropriate agency has been informed and can take action to protect the child when and if this becomes necessary, the family can use this knowledge in a way that increases its ability to control angry impulses.

In some instances, the parent who has abused a child will or can benefit from medication. A depressed client may experience some relief from antidepressant medications. An overly anxious client may experience relief through tranquilizers, and clients who manifest psychotic behaviors can often be helped by major tranquilizers. The medication can often be useful in helping the client temporarily regain control. The use of a homemaker or other social services can sometimes be used to help the family group minimize the effects of environmental stress.

After the family therapist has taken steps to protect the child and help the other family members develop temporary controls, the therapist and the total family group direct their attention toward identifying those family transactions that inhibit the family members' ability to meet each others' psychological needs. In this respect, working with the family group that has developed child abuse signal symptoms is not much different than working with any other family group, except that it is necessary to continue to monitor for the child's safety. For further information on child abuse and some of the patterns that seem to emerge in families that manifest child abuse behavior, the reader should contact the Child Welfare League Of America, 67 Irving Place, New York, New York, 10003.

THE FAMILY IN CRISIS

In many instances the use of a family-centered form of crisis intervention can provide for the family group a viable alternative to the psychiatric hospitalization of one of the family members. In addition, certain forms of family crisis intervention can effectively facilitate change in chronic dysfunctional family interactional patterns in a relatively short period of time. The purpose of this section is to provide a general discussion of some of the concepts and techniques of family crisis intervention therapy reported in family therapy literature that this author has found useful and interesting in the practice of family therapy in a community mental health setting. The two approaches to crisis intervention which will be discussed are (1) the network intervention approach that has been developed by Speck and Attneave and Rueveni (Speck and Attneave, 1971; Speck and Rueveni, 1969) and (2) the family therapy crisis intervention team approach developed by Langsley, Kaplan, Pittman, Machotka, Flomenhaft, and DeYoung (Lansley and Kaplan, 1969).

Network Intervention

The goal of family network intervention is to change dysfunctional family interactions of an acute or chronic nature by "mobilizing family members, relatives, friends and neighbors to meet at the family's home and actively discuss, help and support constructive alternative options available for the family in crisis" (Rueveni and Wiener, 1976). There are six major stages in the network intervention process (Speck and Attneave, 1973):

1. The retribalization stage.
2. The polarization stage.
3. The mobilization for action stage.
4. The depression stage.
5. The breakthrough of the impasse stage.
6. The exhaustion and elation stage.

According to Rueveni (1975), network intervention should not be attempted unless the family is desperate. Without the proper level of desperation in the family group, the family will not be willing to go through the trouble of contacting and arranging with 40 to 50 friends, neighbors, and relatives to meet with the family and the network intervention team at the family's home. If the family group is desperate enough and is able to arrange such a network meeting, the network intervention team will first help those network members present to begin the retribalization process.

In the retribalization process, the network intervention team attempts to help the family network get reacquainted, develop an increased awareness about the client/family's concerns, and develop a sense of network cohesion. This can be facilitated through the use of network activities, such as mingling around, singing, group clapping, as well as other activities that include the entire family network (Rueveni and Speck, 1960).

After retribalization the next process that occurs is polarization. In this stage, various areas of family conflict are manifested in front of the network assembly. This is generally done by having the family members sit in the middle of the network assembly and then share with each other and the network members their problems, concerns, and conflicts. During this stage, different members of the network assembly generally begin to develop empathy for the various family members, and often members of the family network will begin to take sides with various family members. After this has occurred, the network intervention team (from three to six family therapists) will help the network and family members develop network support groups for each member of the family group. This is done by finding activists within the network who are willing to help rather than simply talk about what might be helpful.

The process of finding network activists who are willing to help and then developing support groups for the various family members results in a mobilization for action stage (Rueveni, 1975). During this stage, an effort is mounted by the support groups made up of network activists to find and carry out alternatives that will help the family group members break out of the family crisis. Usually such initial attempts fail and the family network will then move into the depression stage. The depression stage is characterized by setback and an impasse (Rueveni, 1975).

During the depression stage, feelings in the network assembly run high. As the various network members share their feelings of frustration and concern, the network intervention team can often stimulate a breakthrough by the use of encounter group techniques that often exacerbate the energy and feelings in the network meeting (Rueveni and Speck, 1960). Often a network effect will then take over, leading to a real breakthrough of the impasse. The breakthrough of the impasse process then leads to a stage of exhaustion and elation within the family and the total family network. In many instances the approach will be considered so helpful by the family and the network members that they will decide to continue meeting together, even without the presence of the network intervention team, to expand and continue the gains achieved during the network intervention process. For a more detailed description of the network intervention process, the reader is advised to read *Family Networks* by Speck and Atteneave (1973).

The Family Therapy Crisis Intervention Team Approach

The family therapy crisis intervention team approach was developed by Langsley, Kaplan, Pittman, Machotka, Flomenhaft, and DeYoung at the Colorado Psychiatric Hospital in Denver, Colorado. The major goal of the crisis intervention team approach is to prevent psychiatric hospitalization of clients exhibiting acute psychiatric symptoms. This is done through the use of a crisis intervention approach that recognizes the family group as a social unit that has the resources and capacity to manage such symptoms and resolve the stress factors involved in triggering the psychiatric symptoms (Langsley and Kaplan, 1968). The major principles utilized in the family crisis intervention therapy approach include (1) using the patient's expectations of help from the professional; (2) focusing upon the present illness or problem; (3) the use of an active role by the professional team; (4) the use of an eclectic and pragmatic approach by the professional team; (5) enhancing the client's self-esteem; (6) the use of social and environmental manipulation; (7) the use of drugs when necessary; and (8) terminating with the client in a way that leaves the client-family an open door for returning to treatment if this is necessary (Langsley and Kaplan, 1968). These general principles are put into action by the family therapy crisis intervention team by utilizing the following seven techniques of family crisis treatment: (1) immediate aid, (2) defining the crisis as a family problem, (3) focusing on the current crisis, (4) general prescription, (5) specific prescription, (6) identification of role conflicts and renegotiation, and (7) management of future crisis (Langsley and Kaplan, 1968).

Immediate Aid

In the family crisis intervention team approach the family members are seen immediately by at least one of the team members as soon as the family or an individual member of the family makes a request for service. The idea of such a prompt response to a service request is that "the mere promise of help gives the patient and whatever family members are present the conviction that there will be some relief from the tension that has been so troublesome in the immediate past" (Langsley and Kaplan, 1968).

Defining the Crisis as a Family Problem

In addition to providing an immediate service response, the family crisis intervention team also defines for the family group requesting service, from the initial contact, that the present difficulty involves all of the family members and that all family members need to be involved in the treatment process. Also, the treatment team attempts to get other caretakers from the community involved in the treatment process. As a result, in this approach it is not unusual to find ministers, physicians, caseworkers, probation officers, and other community people becoming involved in the family treatment process. Such community helpers are encouraged and invited to work with the family treatment unit as well as to continue their relationships with the family after crisis family therapy is terminated (Langsley and Kaplan, 1968).

Focus on the Current Crisis

In the crisis intervention family therapy team approach, an attempt is made to focus upon the present problem as opposed to looking at problems that have been occurring over a long period of time. In this approach, it is assumed that a recent event has triggered the family's present service request and that what is most helpful to the family group is a resolution of what is troubling the family members currently as opposed to a resolution of concerns that are of a long duration and have a long history. Seeing all the family members helps the crisis team develop a better understanding of what has happened recently to set off the crisis (Langsley and Kaplan, 1968).

General Prescription

A primary goal in the family crisis therapy is to reduce the level of tension in the family group as soon as possible. This can often be done by defining psychiatric symptoms as a way the identified patient is attempting to communicate concerns to the rest of the family group members. At times the use of psychoactive drugs can also reduce tension in the family. Both methods tend to interfere with regression and a further escalation of the family's problem (Langsley and Kaplan, 1968).

Specific Prescription

Specific prescriptions depend upon the unique situation of every family group that requests service. It is assumed that a state of crisis within the family group signals a change in family equilibrium. After the treatment team has decided what events have triggered a state of equilibrium change in the family group, the team will give each family member a set of specific tasks to carry out that are designed to help the family group regain a state of equilibrium (Langsley and Kaplan, 1968).

Identification of Role Conflicts and Renegotiation

During this stage of the intervention process there has generally been an improvement in the identified patient as demonstrated by a reduction in psychiatric symptoms. As this reduction occurs, the focus of treatment changes to include helping the family members discover how the behavior of each family member helped set off the crisis and how each family member can change behavior in a way that would decrease the chance of such a crisis occurring again in the future (Langsley and Kaplan, 1968).

Management of Future Crises

In many instances this type of family crisis approach may help the family members recognize a need for continued treatment centered around long-term interactional problems. If this happens, the family is referred to another agency for further treatment. At other times what is necessary is not a referral for long-term treatment, but rather a termination process that includes telling the family that they can return for treatment if another crisis develops. This is what Langsley and Kaplan (1968) call "termination with an open door." For a further description of the family crises therapy team approach, see Langsley and Kaplan's *The Treatment of Families in Crisis* (1968).

THE SINGLE PARENT FAMILY

It is becoming more and more frequent for the family therapist to receive a service request from a single parent family. Increases in the rate of divorce have resulted in a greater number of family groups in which the children are exposed to more frequent contact with only one of the parents. It has been this author's experience that there are two major forms of single parent family situations that can result in serious family functioning problems for the total family group. These two single parent situation forms can be labeled (1) the assistant parent syndrome, and (2) the "lets keep the fight going by using the kids" syndrome.

The Assistant Parent Syndrome

In the assistant parent syndrome, the single parent assigns one of the children (usually the oldest child) the role of "assistant parent." Duties often include watching the other children when the single parent has to be away from home, making sure that various household chores assigned to the other children are being accomplished, and handling requests made by the other children to visit friends, etc., when the single parent is not available. In many instances such delegation of authority and responsibilities is, in fact, necessary in the single parent family. However, this situation often provides fertile soil for the development of dysfunctional family interactions. For example, in the Rines family, Sue (the mother) has asked Joy (the oldest daughter) to be in charge of the two other children when Sue is away from home. Joy is willing to take this responsibility, but when she is put in charge the other children will then complain to the mother about how Joy is not doing a good job. Sue will then get angry at Joy and yell at her about what Sue believes to be her oldest daughter's mistakes. In this situation, Joy is being placed in a bind. She is asked to take on additional responsibilities in the family and is then not supported in this role by the mother. Also, the mother verbally tells Joy that she feels Joy can do the job, but on another level, by believing the other children's complaints without question and by not supporting Joy, the mother gives Joy an entirely different message. This process allows the two younger children the opportunity to avoid parental control, as neither Joy nor the mother is acting as an effective parent when the mother is away from home. Acting out behavior on the part of the younger children as well as the possibility of somatic complaints by the child in Joy's role will often be the result.

This type of situation can be improved by helping the single parent decide what responsibilities the assistant parental child can, in fact, handle and by then helping the single parent learn to support the parental assistant. In addition, it is often important for the single parent to be very clear to the total family group exactly what are the rights and responsibilities of the assistant parental child. The more clarity that is introduced into this type of situation the better.

The Let's Keep the Marital Fight Going by Using the Kids Syndrome

In the let's keep the marital fight going by using the kids family situation, the parents are divorced or separated but generally do live in the same area. One parent has custody of the children and the other parent has frequent visiting rights. In this situation, the parents continue fighting with each other after they have been separated, but use the children, child rearing issues, visiting rights, and support payments as the focus for maintaining the not yet resolved marital conflict. Very often both parents will attempt to get the children "on my side" and will use the children as "counselors" who will or should listen to the hurt parent's complaints about the spouse. The children are placed in a bind, as both parents may expect the children's loyalty. Acting out behavior and somatic complaints on the part of the children often are signals of the dysfunctional process.

For example, in the Lindsey family the parents are divorced. Lucy (the mother) lives with her two daughters (Sue, age 11, and Peggy, age 13). Bill (the father) lives in the same city and takes the two children for a visit at least once a week. When Bill and Lucy were living together, their interactional process can best be described as attack-avoid. Lucy would nag Bill who in turn would then provide Lucy additional "nagging material" by acting in a passive-aggressive way. Lucy would provide Bill an excuse to act passive-aggressive by her frequent nagging. Even though Bill and Lucy have been divorced for over two years, the interactional pattern continues, only now the parents have started to involve the children in the process. A typical scene occurs as Bill arrives at Lucy's apartment to pick up the two daughters for their weekly visit. He is late as usual and Lucy, who is angry about Bill being late, greets Bill with a few hostile comments about "the support money being late again this month." Bill responds by stating that he will have to bring the children back much earlier than usual the next day (he knows that Lucy has made plans which she will now have to change) and Lucy responds by threatening to not let Bill take the kids after all. The youngest daughter (who has overheard the conversation) begins to develop stomach pains and when she brings this to her mother's attention, Lucy decides that the daughter is, in fact, too sick to go with her father. The oldest daughter runs out of the house slamming the front door as Lucy begins to yell at Bill blaming him for all that has occurred. Bill retreats from the situation and heads to the nearest bar. A few weeks later the family doctor refers the youngest child to a mental health center to get help for her emotional problems.

In such instances, it is imperative to get the divorced parents and the children all in for family therapy. The divorced parents are often very resistive to such an approach, yet without everyone's involvement, very little can usually be done in this type of situation. In general, the divorced parents are very concerned about the children but need to find ways of keeping the parental conflict to themselves. In many instances, the family therapist can obtain the divorced parents' cooperation by stressing the parents' responsibilities to the kids. The goal in this situation is to help the parents learn to maintain the parental conflict within the parental dyad. In many instances, when this has been accomplished, the divorced parents will be able to resolve conflict left over from their marriage. This cannot help but to be of benefit to the children.

SCULPTING THE FAMILY THERAPY SITUATION

In recent years it has become more acceptable for the family therapist to use a wide variety of therapy system compositions to influence the functioning of the total family group. Approaches have been described which range from seeing only one member of the family system to those approaches that include seeing the total family network. In addition, many practitioners recommend the use of individual, group, and milieu therapy approaches to supplement the therapy of the family group or as a part of the family therapy approach. Including the therapist as a participating member of the family therapy system and as a person who is a part of the family process diagnosis adds additional complexity to the total therapy situation. In addition, when we remember that families requesting treatment are often also receiving some form of service from a variety of other professional helpers, a total awareness and understanding of the family's ecological and interactional situation may be very difficult to achieve.

Sculpting the family therapy situation can often help the family therapist to obtain a better idea of what is going on as well as to develop more specific treatment plans, which include therapy system composition decisions and the use of supplemental therapy approaches. The purpose of this section is to illustrate the use of family therapy situation sculpting and to provide a few practical considerations for facilitating the process.

Sculpture Illustration

Carol is a graduate student at Ohio State University who participates in this author's class on marital and family therapy. Her field placement is at a comprehensive mental health center that can provide outpatient, day treatment, and hospital services for clients. Carol was assigned a case where the identified patient (the husband) was complaining about feelings of depression, his fear of becoming violent, and frequent episodes where he has run out of his house leaving his wife and children alone for three or four hours. Carol started seeing the family as a group but was pursuaded by the husband that he needed to see a psychiatrist for medication because he had killed some people in Vietnam and was worried that he might lose control. The referral was made and the psychiatrist immediately hospitalized the husband without consulting with Carol. The psychiatrist diagnosed the husband as having war neurosis and instituted the use of the Pentothal interview to help the husband relieve the trauma experience. This approach did not work and in five weeks the psychiatrist released the husband, who was experiencing increased anxiety, from the hospital for a rest. The psychiatrist continuted to see the husband alone on a weekly basis. While the husband was in the hospital his 16-year-old daughter started running away from home and his 15-year-old daughter was reported by the school as becoming withdrawn and daydreaming all the time. Carol continued to see the wife and children while the husband was in the hospital. Carol continued to serve as the husband's therapist on paper but was not consulted by the psychiatrist on any major discussions. Carol did not feel comfortable talking to the psychiatrist about this, as she believed that her student role would keep her from being heard. At the same time, she continued to have case management responsibility for the husband and the family. Carol asked if she could sculpt this therapy situation in class.

Sculpting the Situation

Carol used the other class participants as sculpting material simulators and sculpted the therapy situation in the following way. The husband was placed in a position where he was leaning on the psychiatrist for support. The husband's head was also turned toward his wife, children, and Carol. The psychiatrist was supporting the husband's weight without any help. The wife was grasping at her two daughters. The 16-year-old daughter was pulling away from mother and the youngest daughter was standing in a position that required the mother's support. Carol was supporting the mother and also was reaching out toward the husband. This position could only be maintained by a great deal of effort on Carol's part. The sculpting can be illustrated in diagram form, as shown in Figure 23.

The sculpture simulation participants were asked to remain "frozen in the sculptive" for five minutes. At the end of this time period each member of the sculpture was asked to report how they felt as a part of the sculpture. The youngest daughter simulator reported that she was feeling isolated and alone. She stated that she did not know whether to follow her older sister or to move closer to her mother. She stated that she started to feel some tension in her stomach toward the end of the time period and that she also felt tired and depressed. The older sister simulator reported that she felt angry and wanted to get out of the situation. She reported that she began to feel tension in her back muscles. The mother simulator stated that she was beginning to get a headache and that she felt a need for support that was not being fulfilled. The husband simulator noted that he felt anxiety and wanted to lean on the psychiatrist simulator for additional support. The psychiatrist simulator reported that he was getting tired and wanted more contact with Carol. Carol stated that she felt confusion and anxiety but that being in the position of supporting the mother and daughters did give her something to do.

The sculpture participants were then asked to rearrange themselves in a way that would be more comfortable for all. They were

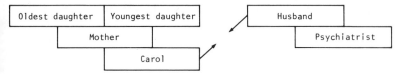

Figure 23.   *The initial sculpture*

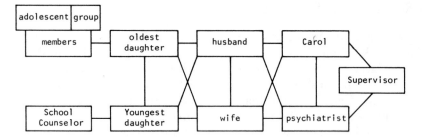

Figure 24. *The second sculpture*

instructed that they could also use resources from the rest of the class, other than just themselves, to build a more comfortable stature. The newly built sculpture can be illustrated in diagram form as is shown in Figure 24.

In the second sculpture, five additional participants were added as well as there being a number of position changes. The sculpture participants decided that it was necessary to move Carol and the psychiatrist together to give them both more support, to move the husband and wife together, and to provide Carol and the psychiatrist a supervisor who could help them work on their relationship. In addition, the oldest daughter was placed in a group and the youngest daughter was sent to a school counselor. All members of the second sculpture found the situation much more confortable. No somatic complaints were recorded. Carol was able to see how the position she had been taking in the situation helped maintain the family and therapy system problems. She found that by moving herself in the sculpture situation, she could create change in the total therapy situation. This insight was used by Carol at her field placement. She talked to the psychiatrist about their relationship; with the psychiatrist's agreement she arranged for their supervision and started seeing the family as a group with the psychiatrist as the co-therapist. She later reported that the husband's signal symptoms had disappeared and that the family was making excellent gains in family therapy. She reported that the sculpture experience was helpful in teaching her the system aspects of the family therapy situation and that it also helped her learn to include herself in the family process diagnosis.

13

A Family Therapy Assessment Guideline

The purpose of this chapter is to provide an outline summary of some of the questions that the family therapist can ask himself in order to help identify what is going on with a particular family and to clarify what forms of intervention might be helpful. The list of questions and assessment areas is somewhat lengthy and as a result, the family therapist should always modify the assessment outline list to fit the needs of the particular clinical situation. It is of questionable value to wait until the therapist can answer all the questions before he begins the intervention process. In addition, much of the therapist's assessment is based upon how the family group members respond to the therapist's interventions. The outline is presented as a guideline rather than a strict set of assessment rules. The outline is presented in a service plan format that this author has found useful in his practice of family therapy in a community mental health setting.

FAMILY THERAPY SERVICE PLAN

I.   General Information
    A. Who are the family members living at home?

B. Who in the family is working? Where? What is their income? Do they enjoy their job?

C. Who in the family is going to school or is in a training program? Where? Do they enjoy it?

D. What is the age and sex of each family member? Who is married to whom? Which kids belong to whom?

E. Where does the family group live? Address? Phone number at home? Work? How can all members be contacted?

F. What family members are not presently living at home? Where do they live? Why did they leave the family home? Are they working? Where? Do they go to school? Where? How often do they see the other family members?

G. What other individuals are an important part or have an important influence on the members of the family group? What is their name? What is their role (i.e., friend, caseworker, lawyer, minister, neighbor, etc.)? Where do they live or where can they be contacted?

II. Referral Source

A. Who referred the family for treatment?

B. Is the family in agreement with the referral?

C. Did the referral source explain that the family would be seen as a group?

D. What was told to the family members about the reason for the referral?

E. Is the person who referred the family for treatment in any form of pain? Would the referral be a way the referral source has of signaling their pain? Would the referral source be included in the treatment? What is the reason for the referral? Who wants what done with whom? Is this realistic?

III. Presenting Problem or Problems

A. What symptoms (i.e., depression, anxiety, delusions, hallucinations) are being manifested? Who in the family is manifesting what symptoms? How does each family member signal his or her pain? Also, what somatic complaints do the various family members talk about? What are all of the signal symptoms and who manifests which signal symptoms?

B. How long have the signal symptoms been occuring? When did they start?

C. Why is the family asking for treatment today? Why not last week? What not last month? Why not last year?

D. What is the sequence of events that led up to the family asking for service or being referred for service?

E. What has the family tried in the past?

F. What resources in the family's social situation have been used or not used?

G. Who else is involved in the problem and who else could help?

H. What is the family's most important present concern? Who in the family is labeled by the family as the identified patient?

IV. Mental Status Information (for each family member)

A. Are the family members all oriented to person, time and place?

B. How is each family member's memory for both recent and remote events? Have any family members experienced trauma injuries to the head? Are there indications of brain tissue impairment?

C. What is the family therapist's estimation of each family member's intelligence? Is each family member functioning at that level? Would an intelligence test help to find out?

D. What is the appearance of each family member?

E. Are delusions or hallucinations noted in the family?

F. Are there any other problems in the mental status of any of the family members? Does the family therapist feel it necessary to give any family member a complete mental status exam? If so, note the results.

G. What are the affect and thought processes of each family member?

H. What is the lethality level of each family member?

I. Did any of the family members come to the family interview under the influence of drugs or alcohol?

V. Family Health Situation and History

A. Do any of the family members have any health problems at present? Are they presently receiving treatment? What kind of treatment? Who is treating the family member with a physical or health problem?

B. Are any of the family members taking medication? If so, who is giving them the medication, what is the medication for, and is the family member taking the medication and taking it in the way it was prescribed? What are the possible side effects of the medication? Could the side effects cause any difficulties in family interaction? Who is monitoring the medication?

C. What is the family's medical history? Does any member have a serious health history? What treatments have been given?

Who followed up on such treatments? What has been the result of such treatment?

D. Are any family members presently complaining of somatic or health problems that have not yet been checked out by a medical examination? If so, why hasn't it been checked out and what plans to do so can be made?

E. Can the family afford the cost of good health care? If not, what plans can be made?

F. What is the family's general attitude toward health care and, if necessary, can this be changed?

VI. Psychiatric History of the Family

A. Have any of the family members ever received counseling, casework, or psychotherapy on an outpatient basis? With whom? Where? When? Were any medications or somatic treatments used? What medication? What other treatment?

B. Have any of the family members or relatives ever been admitted to a psychiatric hospital? If so, where, when, how long, what medications and somatic treatments were used, and was there any follow-up?

C. Have any of the family members or relatives ever received any form of payment for a psychiatric disability? If so, how much of a disability and for what period of time?

VII. Educational, Training, and Employment Situation

A. What is the educational level of the various family members?

B. What forms of special training have the various family members received?

C. What family members are working?

D. What family members are in school?

E. Can anything be done to help the family upgrade its educational and employment situation?

VIII. Social Service Inquiry

A. Does the family have adequate financial resources, housing, food, transportation, and health care?

B. Is the family in need of any specialized services, such as recreation, socialization activities, etc?

C. What social resources have been used with the family, what resources are not available to the family, and what additional resources can be used?

IX. Family Life-Cycle Stage

A. What stage of family life-cycle development is this family engaged in? Is it a beginning family (married couple without children)? Is it a childbearing family (oldest child up to thirty months)? Is it a preschool family (oldest child up to six years)? Is it a school age family (oldest child six to thirteen years)? Is it a family with teen-age children? Is it a family with children leaving (first child gone through last child leaving the family)? Is it a family without any children still at home (marital pair working toward retirement)? Is it an aging family (husband and wife retired, to death of both spouses)?

B. What family life-cycle tasks are the family members working on and how are the family members accomplishing these tasks? Which tasks are difficult for the family group to achieve and how can the family therapist help?

X. Family Interaction

A. How do the family members send messages to each other? Are such messages clear, precise, and congruent? What is the family style in terms of coding operations? What dysfunctional coding operation games do the various family members play? What coding operation myths are acted out in the family interactions? What coding operation rules are verbalized by the family members and how is this different from what actually happens?

B. How do the family members evaluate and receive the messages they get from each other? Are such cognitive decoding evaluations in tune with objective reality? Are they life-preserving, goal-producing, and do they tend to decrease dysfunctional conflict with both self and other? What is the family style in terms of decoding operations? What decoding games do the various family members play? What decoding myths and rules get acted out in family interaction and are they different than the rules that are verbalized by the family members?

C. What is the family structure for the family communication flow? Does the family group exhibit a balanced or unbalanced family structure? Do the parents work together to give direction to the rest of the family group? Is there an effective generational boundary between the parents and the children, and between the parents and their parents? Are such boundaries open enough so that information flow and communication can cross boundaries? Are there any rigid coalitions in the family that result in an unbalanced family structure?

D. How do the various family members reinforce their own and each other's transactional style? Do the family members reinforce functional transactions? How is this done in the family?

Do the family members reinforce dysfunctional transactions and how is this done? What transactions that occur in the family are complementary? How is reciprocity operationalized in this particular family group?

E. How do the family members manifest themselves to the other family members, allow other family members to manifest themselves, and how does the family negotiate with each other for joint relationship outcomes?

F. How does the family group interact with other segments of society? Is the boundary between the family and society overly rigid or permeable? Is there a family spokesperson? How does this work? Does the spokesperson do an effective job?

XI. Family Treatment Intervention Plan

A. What interventions can the family therapist use that will increase the family's ability to obtain any social service resources that would help the family group function in a more effective way? How can the therapist evaluate whether or not such interventions have been effective and useful?

B. What interventions can the family therapist use that will increase the individual capacities in all functioning areas for all family members? How can the therapist evaluate whether or not such interventions have been effective and useful?

C. What is the transaction history of the family group and will the family members use this history in either a positive or negative way to inhibit or enhance the family treatment process? If negative, how can this be minimized and, if positive, how can this be used most effectively?

D. What interventions can the family therapist use that will improve the quality of the family transactional style? How will such interventions improve family coding, decoding, and family structure? How will such interventions interrupt dysfunctional reciprocity? How can the therapist measure whether or not such interventions have been effective and useful?

E. What plans for follow-up have been made to evaluate the effects of family therapy? How soon should follow-up occur with the family and what should be measured at the time of follow-up?

XII. Other Assessment Considerations

A. Should any family members be referred for psychological testing? If so, what is to be gained and what is it that the family therapist wants to know?

B. Should any family member be referred to a psychiatrist for evaluation? If so, what is to be gained and what does the family therapist want the psychiatrist to do or find out?
C. Should the family therapist make a home visit? If so, why? What is to be gained and what does the family therapist hope to accomplish or hope to find out?
D. Should any family members be referred for some form of additional therapy (i.e., group therapy, individual therapy, speech therapy, etc.) and what does the family therapist hope to accomplish by such a referral?
E. Is the therapist involved with the family in a way that will help the family continue the problems? How can the therapist monitor for this?

SOME FINAL NOTES

Throughout this volume I have attempted to make clear a family-oriented helping process that I believe can be very useful to the professional helping practitioner. The family approach includes a way of understanding emotional distress, a way of developing appropriate intervention strategies, and more than any other therapeutic approach, allows a person the opportunity to act out and practice more enjoyable forms of relating and existing in a natural setting. Family therapy is an effective and efficient way of helping people. Its principles are applicable to a wide variety of human concerns, and significant therapeutic gains can occur in a relatively short period of time. Whether the professional helper is working in a clinic, hospital, public assistance program, private practice, family service agency, court, or mental health facility, he is confronted daily by families that exhibit emotional problems and concerns. In view of this practice reality, it is my sincere hope that this book will stimulate additional interest in the field of family therapy.

Bibliography

Ackerman, N. 1968. *The Psychodynamics of Family Life*. New York: Basic Books.

Ackerman, N. 1966. *Treating the Troubled Family*. New York: Basic Books.

Andrews, E. 1976. Personal communication.

Andrews, E. 1974. *The Emotionally Disturbed Family*. New York: Jason Aronson.

Andrews, E. 1973. Family therapy. In *Group Therapy for the Adolescent, eds*, N. Brandes, and M. Gradner, New York: Jason Aronson.

Andrews, E. 1972. Conjoint psychotherapy with married couples and families. *Cincinnati J. Med.* 53:318–19.

Andrews, E. 1965. "Identity maintenance operations and group therapy process. *Int. J. Group Psychother.* 15:491–99.

Ard, B., and Ard, C., eds. 1969. *Handbook of Marriage Counseling*. Palo Alto, Calif.: Science and Behavior Books.

Bandler, R., and Grinder, J. 1975. *The Structure of Magic*, vols. I and II. Palo Alto, Calif.: Science and Behavior Books.

Bandura, A. 1971. Psychotherapy based upon modeling principles. In *Handbook of Psychotherapy and Behavior Change*, eds. A. E. Bergin and S. L. Garfield. New York: John Wiley and Sons.

Bateson, G. 1967. *Naven*. Stanford: Stanford University Press.

Bateson, G. 1958. Schizophrenic distortion of communication. In *Psychotherapy of Chronic Schizophrenic Patients*, ed. C. Whitaker. Boston: Little, Brown.

Bell, J. 1961. *Family Group Therapy*. U. S. Public Health Monograph No. 64. Washington, D.C.: U.S. Government Printing Office.

Bell, N., and Vogel, E., eds. 1960. *A Modern Introduction to the Family*. Glencoe, Ill.: Free Press.

Berne, E. 1964. *Games People Play*. New York: Grove Press.

Birdwhistell, R. 1960. *Essays on Body Motion Communication*. Philadelphia: University of Pennsylvania Press.

Block, D. 1973. *Techniques of Family Psychotherapy, A Primer*. New York: Grune and Stratton.

Bodin, A., and Farber, A. 1973. How to go beyond the use of language. In *The Book of Family Therapy*, eds. A. Farber, M. Mendelsohn, and A. Napier, Boston: Houghton-Mifflin Co.

Borzormenyi-Nagy, I., and Framo, J. eds. *Intensive Family Therapy*. New York: Harper and Row.

Borzormenyi-Nagy, I., and Zuk, G. eds. 1967. *Family Therapy and Disturbed Families*. Palo Alto, Calif.: Science and Behavior Books.

Bowen, M. 1961. Family psychotherapy. *Am. J. Orthopsychiatry* 31:40–60.

Bowen, M. 1969. A family concept of schizophrenia. In *The Etiology of Schizophrenia*, ed. D. Jackson. New York: Basic Books.

Coser, R., ed. 1964. *The Family, Its Structure and Functions*. New York: St. Martin's Press.

Curry, A. 1966. The family therapy situation as a system. *Family Process* 5:131–141

Duhl, F., Kantor, D., and Duhl, B. 1973. Learning, space, and action in family therapy: a primer sculpture. In *Techniques of Family Psychotherapy: A Primer*, ed. D. Block. New York: Grune and Stratton.

Duvall, E. 1967. *Family Development*. Philadelphia: Lippincott.

Ellis, A. 1962. *Reason and Emotion in Psychotherapy*. New York: Lyle Stuart.

Farber, A., Mendelsohn, M., and Napier, A. 1973. *The Book of Family Therapy*. Boston: Houghton-Mifflin.

Farrelly, F., and Brandsma, J. 1974. *Provocative Therapy*. Ft. Collins, Colorado: Shields.

Fix, J., and Haffke, E. 1976. *Basic Psychological Therapies*. New York: Human Sciences Press.

Flommenhaft, K., and Kaplan, D. 1968. Clinical significance of current kinship relationships. *Social Work* 13:68–75.

Glick, I., and Kessler, D. 1974. *Marital and Family Therapy*. New York: Grune and Stratton.

Goode, W. 1964. *The Family*. Englewood Cliffs, N.J.: Prentice-Hall.

Green, B. L., ed. 1965. *The Psychotherapies of Marital Dysharmony*. New York: Free Press.

Green, S., and Regensburg, J. 1956. Casework diagnosis of marital problems. In *Neurotic Interaction in Marriage*, ed. V. Eisenstein. New York: Basic Books.

Greenberg, L. 1975. Therapeutic grief work with children. *Social Casework* 56:396–403.

Group for the Advancement of Psychiatry. 1970. *The Field of Family Therapy*. New York: GAP.

Guerin, P. ed. 1976. *Family Therapy*. New York: Gardner Press, Inc.

Haas, W. 1965. The intergenerational encounter: a method in treatment. *Social Work* 13:92–101.

Haley, J. 1963. *Strategies of Psychotherapy*. New York: Grune and Stratton.

Haley, J. 1967. Toward a theory of pathological famillies. In *Family Therapy and Disturbed Families*, eds. I. Berzormenyi- Nagy, and G. Zuk. Palo Alto: Science and Behavior Books.

Haley, J. 1970. Approaches to family therapy. *Int. J. Psychiatry* 9:233–242.

Haley, J. ed. 1971. *Changing Families*. New York: Grune and Stratton.

Haley, J. 1972. Family Therapy. In *Progress in Group and Family Therapy*, eds. C. Sager, and H. Kaplan. New York: Brunner/Mazel.

Haley, J. 1976. *Problem Solving Therapy*. San Francisco: Jossey-Bass.

Haley, J., and Hoffman, LK. 1967. *Techniques of Family Therapy*. New York: Basic Books.

Harris, T. 1967. *I'm Ok, You're Ok*. New York: Harper and Row.

Helfer, R., and Kempe, H. 1972. *Helping the Battered Child and His Family*. Philadelphia: J.B. Lippincott Co.

Hoffman, L. 1976. Breaking the homeostatic cycle. In *Family Therapy*, ed. P. Guerin. New York: Gardner Press, Inc.

Holmes, S., Barhart, C., Cantoni, L., and Reymer, E. 1973. Working with the parent in child abuse cases. *Social Casework* 56:3–12.

Jackson, D., 1967. *Human Communication*, vol. *I* and *II*. Palo Alto, Calif.: Science and Behavior Books.

Jackson, D., and Lederer, W. 1969. *Mirages of Marriage*. New York: Weston.

Kempler, W. 1974. *Principles of Gestalt Family Therapy*. Salt Lake City: Desert Press.

Knisley, M., and Bussell, J. 1977. *Southwest Community Mental Health Center Aftercare Proposal*. Operations Grant submitted to the National Institute of Mental Health.

Laing, R. D. 1965. Mystification, confusion and conflict. In *Intensive Family Therapy*, eds. I. Borzormeyni-Nagy and J. Framo. New York: Harper and Row.

Laing, R. D., and Esterson, S. 1969. Families and schizophrenia. *Int. J. of Psychiatry* 4:65–71.

Langsley, D., and Kaplan, D. 1968. *The Treatment of Families in Crisis*. New York: Grune and Stratton.

Lantz , J. 1975. The rational treatment of parental adjustment reaction to adolescence. *Clinical Social Work J*. 3(2):100–108.

Lantz, J. 1977. Family therapy: using a transactional approach. *J. Psychiatr. Nurs*. 15(4): 17–22.

Lantz, J. 1978. Co-therapy approach in family therapy. *Social Work* 23(2):156–58.

Lantz, J., and Boer, A. 1974. "Adolescent group therapy membership selection. *Clinical Social Work Journal* 2(3): 172–181.

Lantz, J., and Lenahan, B. 1976. Referral fatigue therapy. *Social Work* 21(3): 239–240.

Luthman, S., and Kirschenbaum, M. 1974. *The Dynamic Family*. Palo Alto, Calif.: Science and Behavior Books.

Marcus, L. 1974. Communication concepts and principles. In *Social Work Treatment*, ed. F. Turner. New York: The Free Press.

Marujama, M. 1963. The second cybernetics—deviation amplifying mutual causative processes. *American Scientist* 51:164–179.

Masters, W., and Johnson, V. 1970. *Human Sexual Inadequacy*. Boston: Little, Brown.

Maultsby, M. 1975. *Help Yourself to Happiness*. Boston: Marborough House.

Minuchin, S. 1974. *Families and Family Therapy*. Cambridge: Harvard University Press.

Minuchin, S., Montalvo, B., Gurney, G., Rosman, B., and Schumer, F. 1967. *Families of the Slums*. New York: Basic Books.

Mooney, R. 1963. A conceptual model for integrating four approaches to the identification of creative talent, eds. C. Taylor, and F. Barron. In *Scientific Creativity: Its Recognition and Development*. New York: John Wiley and Sons.

Mullan, H., and Sangiuliano, I. 1946. *The Therapist's Contribution to the Treatment Process*. Springfield, Ill.: Charles C. Thomas.

Paul, W., and Paul, B. 1975. *A Marital Puzzle*. New York: W. W. Norton.

Paul, W. 1967.The use of empathy in the resolution of grief. *Perspect. Biol. Med.* II:153–169.

Pittman, F., and Flomenhaft, K. 1970. Treating the doll's house marriage. *Family Process* 9:143–155.

Pollak, O., and Friedman, A., eds. 1969. *Family Dynamics and Female Sexual Delinquency*. Palo Alto, Calif.: Science and Behavior Books.

Rueveni, U. 1975. Network intervention with a family in crisis. *Family Process* 14(2):193-203.

Rueveni, U., and Speck, R. 1960. Using encounter techniques in the treatment of social network of the schizophrenic family. *Int. J. Group Psychother.* 19:495–500.

Rueveni, U., and Wiener, M. 1976. Network intervention of disturbed families: the key role of network activists. *Psychotherapy* 13(2):173–176.

Sager, C. 1968. An overview of family therapy. *Int. J. Group Psychother.* 18:302–308.

Sager, C., and Kaplan, H., 1972. *Progress in Group and Family Therapy*. New York: Brunner/Mazel.

Satir, V. 1963. Schizophrenia and family therapy. In *Social Work Practice*. Published for the National Conference on Social Welfare, New York: Columbia University Press.

Satir, V. 1964. *Conjoint Family Therapy*. Palo Alto, Calif: Science and Behavior Books.

Satir, V. 1968. Conjoint marital therapy. In *The Psychotherapies of Marital Disharmony*, ed. B. L. Green. New York: Free Press.

Satir, V. 1972. *Peoplemaking*. Palo Alto, Calif.: Science and Behavior Books.

Scherz, F. 1970. Theory and practice of family therapy. In *Theories of Social Casework*, eds., R. Roberts, and R. Nee. Chicago: University of Chicago Press.

Sherman, S. 1974. Family therapy. In *Social Work Treatment*, ed. F. Turner. New York: The Free Press.

Simon, R. 1972. Sculpting the family. *Family Process* II49-58.

Smoyak, S. ed. 1975. *The Psychiatric Nurse as a Family Therapist*. New York: John Wiley and Sons.

Speck, R., and Attneave, C. 1971. Social network intervention. In *Changing Families*, ed. J. Haley. New York: Grune and Stratton.

Speck, R., and Attneave, C. 1973. *Family Networks*. New York: Pantheon Books.

Speck, R., and Rueveni, U. 1969. Network therapy, a developing concept. *Family Process* 8:182–191.

Tosi, D. 1974. *Youth Toward Personal Growth: A Rational Emotive Approach*. Columbus, Ohio: Charles E. Merrill.

Truax, C.B., and Mitchell, K.M. 1971. Research on certain therapist interpersonal skills in relation to process and outcome. In *Handbook of Psychotherapy and Behavior Change*, eds. A.E. Bergin and S.L. Garfield. New York: John Wiley and Sons.

Vorland, A. 1962. *Family Casework Diagnosis*. New York: Columbia University Press.

Watzlawick, P. 1966. A structured family interview. *Family Process* 5:108–116.

Watzlawick, P., Beavin, J., and Jackson, D. 1967. *Pragmatics of Human Communication*. New York: W.W. Norton.

Watzlawick, P., Weakland, J., and Fisch, R. 1974. *Change*. New York: W.W. Norton.

Wender, P. 1968. Vicious and virtuous circles: the role of deviation amplifying feedback in the origin and perpetuation of behavior. *Psychiatry* 31:309–324.

Wynne, L., Ryckoff, I., Day, J., and Hersch, S. 1958. Pseudomutuality in the family relations of schizophrenics. *Psychiatry* 21:205–220.

Zuk, G. 1971. Family therapy. In *Changing Families*, ed. J. Haley. New York: Grune and Stratton.

Zuk, G. 1971. *Family Therapy: A Triadic Based Approach*. New York: Behavioral Publications.

Zwerling, I., and Mendelsohn, M. 1965. Initial family reactions to day hospitalization. *Family Process* 4:50–63.

Index

A

Acceptance of symptoms, 17
Aftercare families, 181–85
Assessment, 23, 31–32
  marbles test procedure, 33
  plan a picnic procedure, 32
  projective procedure, 32
Assessment guidelines, 201–207
Assistant parent syndrome, 195–96

B

Balanced family group, 11–12
Blindness in a family group, 177–81
Boundary setting, 47–50
Breakthrough of impasse stage, 191

C

Child abuse, 185–89
Clarification of communication, 36–38
Closed system, 40, 41
Coalitions in co-therapy, 163–65
Communication in family group, 3–5
Co-therapy
  disadvantages of, 159–60
  effects on support and confrontation, 160–61
  modeling approaches for, 41, 161–62
  opportunities for therapeutic coalitions, 163–64
  supervision in, 162–63
  use of one-way mirror, 163
Crisis intervention, 189–90. *See also* Single parent family therapy
  network intervention, 190–92
  team approach, 192–94